Historical Materialism
For Everyone

by

Herman Gorter

Edited Jamshid R. Davis

Omnia Sunt Communia Press
Northview, MO
2023

Originally published in 1908

Original title "Historical Materialism for Workers"

978-1-312-55870-0

Imprint: Lulu.com

Table of Contents

I. The Theme of this Book

Social democracy embraces not merely the aspiration to transform private property in the means of production, that is, natural forces and instruments of labor, as well as the soil, into common property, and to achieve this thanks to the political struggle, to the conquest of State power; social democracy embraces not just a political and economic struggle; it is more: it also embraces a struggle of ideas over a conception of the world, a struggle fought against the possessing classes.

The worker who wants to help defeat the bourgeoisie and bring his class to power must eliminate from his mind the bourgeois ideas which have been inculcated in him since his childhood by the State and the Church. It is not enough to join the trade union and the political party. He will never be able to be victorious with them if he does not transform himself internally into a different human being than the one molded by his rulers. There is a certain conception, a conviction, a philosophy, one might say, which the bourgeoisie rejects but which the worker must embrace if he wants to defeat the bourgeoisie.

The bourgeoisie want to convince the workers that the mind is above material social existence, that the mind alone rules and forms matter. They have been using the mind as a means of domination: they have science, law, politics, art and the Church behind them and their rule incorporates all of these things. Now they want to make the workers believe that this is an expression of the natural order; that mind by its nature rules over material social existence, that it rules over the workers in the factory, the mine, the farm, the railroad, and the ship. The worker who believes this, who believes that mind creates production, labor and social classes by itself, this worker submits to the bourgeoisie and their accomplices, the priests, the experts, etc., because the bourgeoisie controls most of the sciences, it controls the Church, and thus mind, and, if this is true, it must rule.

To preserve its power, the possessing class is trying to convince the workers to accept this as true. But the worker who wants to become a free being, who wants to place the State under the power of his class and seize the means of production from the possessing classes, this worker must understand that the bourgeoisie, with its way of depicting things, turns them on their head and that it is not mind which determines existence, but social existence which determines mind.

If the worker understands this, then he will free himself from the mental rule of the possessing classes and will oppose their way of thinking with his own more just and more resilient way of thinking.

Furthermore, because social evolution and social existence itself are moving in the direction of socialism, because they are paving the way for socialism, the worker who understands this and who understands that his socialist thinking comes from social existence, will recognize that what is happening all around him in human society is the cause of what is produced in his head, that socialism is born in his head because it is growing outside, in society. He will recognize and will feel that he possesses the truth about reality; this will give him the courage and the confidence that are necessary for the social revolution.

This understanding is therefore just as indispensable for proletarian combat as the trade union and the political struggle; one could say that without this knowledge the economic and political struggles could not be carried through to the end. Mental slavery prevents the worker from correctly prosecuting the material struggle; a poor proletarian, his consciousness of being mentally stronger than his masters raises him above them and confers upon him the power to defeat them.

Historical materialism is the doctrine which explains that it is social existence which determines the mind, and which obliges thought to take particular paths and which thus determines the will and the acts of individuals and classes.

In this pamphlet we shall attempt to prove to the workers, as simply and as clearly as possible, the truth of this doctrine.

II. What Historical Materialism Is Not

However, before we proceed to a clear statement of what historical materialism is, in anticipation of encountering certain prejudices and foreseeable misunderstandings, we would like to first of all say what historical materialism is not. For besides the historical materialism that is the doctrine of social democracy, a particular doctrine established by Friedrich Engels and Karl Marx, there is also philosophical materialism, and various systems of that kind. And these systems, unlike historical materialism, do not address the question of how the mind is compelled by social existence, by the mode of production, technology, and labor, to proceed by way of determined paths, but rather the question of the relation between body and mind, matter and soul, God and the world, etc. These other systems, which are not historical but merely philosophical, attempt to find an answer to the question: what is the nature of the relationship between thinking in general and matter, or, how did thinking arise? Historical materialism, on the other hand, asks: why is it that, in any particular era, thought takes on one form or another? General philosophical materialism will say, for example: matter is eternal, and mind is born from it under certain conditions; it then disappears when its conditions no longer exist; while historical materialism will say: the fact that proletarians think in a different way than the possessing classes is a consequence of such-and-such causes.

General philosophical materialism asks about the nature of thought. Historical materialism asks about the causes of changes in thought. The former tries to explain the origin of thought, the latter its evolution. The former is philosophical, the latter historical. The former assumes a context in which there is no thought, no mind; the latter assumes the existence of mind. The big difference is apparent.

Those who want to examine and learn to understand the doctrine of social democracy must begin by paying particular attention to this difference. For their opponents, and especially all the religious believers, want at all costs to confound the two systems and, because of the revulsion expressed by the religious workers for the former doctrine, to banish the other system as well. The pastors of the churchgoers say: materialism proclaims that the entire world is nothing but matter in mechanical motion, that matter and force are the only things that absolutely and eternally exist, that thought is simply a secretion of the brain, just as bile is a secretion of the liver; they say that the materialists are worshippers of matter and that historical materialism is the same thing as philosophical materialism. Many workers, especially in the Catholic regions, which still cling to the servile adoration of the spirit and where those who are acquainted with the true ideas of social democracy concerning the nature of mind, as they have been presented by Joseph Dietzgen, are few and far between, heed these warnings and are afraid to listen to social democratic speakers who want to lead them to the worship of matter and thus to eternal damnation.

These claims are false. We shall show, by means of a series of examples, that historical materialism does not address the general relationship between mind and matter, soul and body, God and the world, thought and existence, but only explains the changes which thought undergoes and which are produced by social transformations.

But if we prove that historical materialism is not the same thing as philosophical materialism, we do not thereby intend to imply that historical materialism cannot lead to a general conception of the world. To the contrary, historical materialism is, like every empirical science, a means to reach a general philosophical conception of the world. This is an especially important aspect of its meaning for the proletariat. It brings us closer to a general representation of the world. This representation is not, however, that of the mechanical-material view, any more than it is that of the catholic-christian, evangelical or liberal view; it is another conception altogether, a new conception, a new vision of the world which is particular to social democracy. Historical materialism is not a conception of the world strictly speaking; it is a path, a means, one of many means to reach such a conception, like Darwinism, all the sciences, Marx's doctrine of capital and Dietzgen's doctrine of mind, or the knowledge of such means. Any one of these means alone is not enough to attain this conception of the world but all of them together lead to it.

Since we shall only be discussing historical materialism in this pamphlet, we shall obviously not speak in any detail about the general philosophical conception of social democracy. In relation to some of the examples which shall help shed light on our topic, we shall nevertheless encounter opportunities to display a glimpse of this general conception of the world, so that the reader may acquire some understanding of this totality of which historical materialism constitutes one part alongside so many other sciences.

III. The Content of the Doctrine

What, then, is the general content of our doctrine? Before we start to demonstrate its accuracy and its truth, we shall first provide the reader with a clear general outline of what we intend to prove.

For anyone who observes the social life which surrounds him it is obvious that society's members live in certain mutual relations. They are not social equals but occupy higher or lower ranks and are opposed to one another in groups or classes. The superficial observer might think that these relations are nothing but property relations: some possess the land, others the factories, the means of transport or commodities destined for sale, while others possess nothing. Or he might think that the difference is principally a political difference; certain groups have the power of the State at their disposal, others have little or no influence over the State. But the more penetrating observer sees that, behind property and political relations, there are production relations, that is, relations in which men confront one another in the production of society's needs.

Workers, businessmen, ship-owners, rentiers, big landowners, farmers, wholesalers, and shopkeepers are what they are due to the place they occupy in the production process, in the transformation and circulation of products. This difference is even more profound than the distinction between someone with money and someone without money. The transformation of the wealth of nature is the basis of society. We are reciprocally involved in relations of labor and production.

On what, then, are these labor relations based? Are all men, as capitalists and workers, big landowners, farmers and day laborers, somehow simply floating in the air, so they can all call each other members of society?

No, labor relations are based on technology, on the instruments with which the land and nature are transformed. Industrialists and proletarians rely upon machinery, they are dependent on machinery. If there were no machines, there would be no industrialists or proletarians, or at least not the kind we know today.

The occupation of the artisan weaver gave birth to work at home for the whole family; the occupation of weaver in a small workshop engendered a society of small masters and clerks; large-scale steel weaving machinery powered by steam or electricity led to a society of great industrialists, stockbrokers, directors, bankers and wage workers.

Production relations are not suspended in the air like clouds of smoke or steam; they form solid boundaries within which men are enclosed. The production process is a material process; its instruments are the walls and foundations of the space we occupy.

Technology, the instruments of production and the productive forces comprise society's infrastructure, the real basis upon which the whole gigantic highly developed organism of society is raised. But the same men who establish their social relations based on their mode of production also form their ideas, representations, concepts and principles on the basis of these relations. The capitalists, the workers, and the other classes who, as a result of the technology of the society in which they live, are obliged to confront one another in specific relations—as master and servant, property owner and the propertyless, landowner, farmer, and day laborer—these same capitalists, workers, etc., also think as capitalists, workers, etc. They form their ideas and representations not as abstract beings, but as real, living, quite concrete men; they are social men who live in a specific society.

Therefore, it is not just our material relations which depend on technology, and are based on labor and the productive forces, but also, since we think within these material relations and under these relations, our thoughts depend directly on these relations and thus indirectly on the productive forces.

The modern social existence of the proletariat was created by machines. The proletariat's social thoughts, which result from the relation in which the proletariat as such finds itself, are then indirectly based on the modern replacement of labor by machinery, they indirectly depend on it. And the same is true of all the classes of capitalist society. For the relations within which individual men confront one another are not just applicable to each man individually. Socially, each man is not situated in a unique relation which applies to him as a personal fact as opposed to other men; he has many fellow men who are in the same relation with each other. A worker—to continue with this example—is not alone as a wage worker in relation to other men, he is one of numerous wage workers, he is a member of a class of millions of wage workers who, as wage workers, find themselves in the same situation. And the same is true of all men in the civilized world; everyone belongs to a group, a class whose members are involved in the same way in the production process. Therefore, not only is it true that a worker, a capitalist, a peasant, etc., will think socially as the work relations make them think, but their ideas and representations will coincide in their principal characteristics with those of hundreds of thousands of other people who find themselves in the same situation as them. There is a class thought, just as there is a class position in the labor process.

The form—here we continue to occupy ourselves with the general outline of our doctrine—in which the work relations of the different classes (capitalists, businessmen, workers, etc.) are revealed is at the same time a property relation in capitalist society and, in general, in any society divided into classes. The capitalists, the wage workers, the shopkeepers and the peasants not only occupy their own positions within production, but also in terms of possession, of property. The shareholder who pockets the dividends plays in the production process not just the role of supplier of money and parasite, but also the role of co-owner of the business, the means of production, the land, the tools, the raw materials and the products. The shopkeeper is not only someone who participates in exchange, an intermediary, but is also an owner of commodities and of commercial profit. The worker is not merely the person who makes the goods, but is also the owner of his labor power, which he sells in each instance, and of the price which his labor power fetches. In these terms, work relations, in a society which is divided into classes, are at the same time property relations.

It has not always been so. In primitive communist society, the land, the communally built dwelling, the herds, in a word, the principal means of production, were common property. Essential social labor was carried out jointly; setting aside gender and age distinctions, there was equality in the production process and there was little or no difference in the control of property.

But after the division of labor advanced so far that all kinds of special jobs were created, and, thanks to an improved technology and a more developed division of labor, after a surplus above and beyond what was immediately needed for survival was produced, certain eminent professions—distinguished by knowledge or valor—such as those of priest and warrior, succeeded in appropriating this surplus and, ultimately, the means of production as well. This is how classes were born and this is how private property became the form in which labor relations have been manifested.

"Thanks to the development of technology and the division of labor, classes were created. Class relations and property relations rest upon labor. Thanks to the development of technology, which has placed certain professions in a position to take possession of the means of production, the propertied and propertyless were born and most of the people were transformed into slaves, serfs and wage workers."

And the surplus which technology and labor produce beyond what is immediately needed has become increasingly important, and so has the wealth of the owners, and all the more stark is the class contrast for those who have no property. And, therefore, the class struggle has grown proportionately, the struggle waged by the classes for the possession of the products and means of production and has thus become the general form of the struggle for existence of men in society. Labor relations are property relations, and property relations are relations between classes which are engaged in struggle with one another; and all these relations, taken as a whole, rest upon the development of labor, they result from the labor process and technology.

But technology does not stand still. It is part of a faster or slower development and movement, the forces of production grow, the mode of production changes. And when the mode of production changes, the relations in which men face one another must necessarily change as well. The relations of the old small-scale master craftsmen among themselves and with their apprentices are completely different from the present-day relations of the big business owners among themselves and with the wage-earning proletariat. Mechanized production has resulted in a modification of the old relations. And since, in a class society, production relations are at the same time property relations, the latter are revolutionized along with the former. And since conceptions, representations, ideas, etc. are formed within the framework and as functions of the relations in which men live, consciousness is also modified when labor, production and property undergo changes.

Labor and thought are parts of a continuous process of change and development. "By transforming nature by means of his labor, man simultaneously transforms his own nature." The mode of production of material life conditions all of social life. "It is not man's consciousness which determines his existence, but his social existence which determines his consciousness."

At a certain stage of development, however, the material productive forces of society enter into conflict with the existing relations of production and property. The new productive forces cannot develop within the old relations; they cannot fully unfold within them. A struggle then begins between those who have an interest in preserving the old relations of production and property and those who have an interest in the development of the new productive forces. An era of social revolution ensues and lasts until the new productive forces are victorious and new relations of production and property arise in which the new productive forces can flourish.

And, by way of this revolution, man's thought changes as well; it is modified with and within this revolution.

I have briefly summarized the content of our doctrine. It can be recapitulated in an outline form as follows:

I. Technology, the productive forces, forms the basis of society.

The productive forces determine the relations of production, the relations in which men confront one another in the production process.

The relations of production are at the same time property relations.

The relations of production and property are not only relations between persons, but between classes.

These relations of class, property, and production (in other words, social existence) determine man's consciousness, that is, his conceptions of rights, politics, morality, religion, philosophy, art, etc.

II. Technology is undergoing continuous development.

Consequently, the productive forces, the mode of production, property, and class relations, are also undergoing constant modification.

Therefore, man's consciousness, his conceptions and representations of rights, politics, morality, religion, philosophy, art, etc., are also modified along with the relations of production and the productive forces.

III. The new technology, at a certain stage of development, enters into conflict with the old relations of production and property.

Finally, the new technology prevails.

The economic struggle between the conservative sectors which have an interest in the preservation of the old forms and the progressive sectors which have an interest in the rise of the new forces enters consciousness under juridical, political, religious, philosophical and artistic forms.

Now we shall attempt to prove that our theory is correct. By means of a series of examples we shall demonstrate the causal relation between changes in human technology and changes in human thought. If we succeed in doing so, then we shall have toppled an important pillar upon which the power of the capitalists over the workers rests. We shall thus have proven that no divine providence or human mental superiority can prevent the workers from ruling the world when technology transforms them into intellectual and material masters.

IV Our Examples

The examples we shall provide below, first, must be very simple. They must be understood by workers who have little historical knowledge. They must thus possess a persuasive force because of their clarity. We shall therefore choose large-scale, wide-ranging phenomena, whose effects are visible everywhere.

If our doctrine is correct, it must obviously be valid for all of history.

It must be able to explain all class struggles, all radical changes in the thought of classes and society.

A great deal of historical knowledge, however, is required to explain, based on our doctrine, examples drawn from previous centuries. We shall show how dangerous it is to want to apply our doctrine to eras or situations concerning which we have little or no knowledge. Neither the reader nor the author of this pamphlet possesses such extensive historical knowledge. We shall therefore only provide very simple examples, but we shall seek them primarily in our own era; large-scale phenomena which every worker knows or could know from his environment, changes in social relations and social thought which must be noticed by every living man. Questions, in short, which are of the greatest interest for the existence of the working class and which can only be satisfactorily resolved for that class by social democracy.

Furthermore, we shall have in this manner simultaneously conducted good propaganda work.

But very important and seemingly powerful arguments will be presented against our doctrine.

This is why, when we are discussing all kinds of mental phenomena, such as changes in political ideas, religious representations and other similar facts, we shall pause to consider and to combat on each occasion one of the most significant arguments of our opponents, so that our doctrine can be progressively approached from every angle and a good view of the whole can be obtained.

The material modifications brought about by technological change can quite easily be distinguished. In every industrial sector, in the means of transportation and in agriculture, too, everywhere technology is changing, the productive forces are changing. We see this taking place every day before our eyes.

Typesetting and the manufacture of printed materials were until recently still generally done by hand. But technological progress has brought the linotype machine, which selects the letters in obedience to the hand of the typographer and puts them in their place.

Glassblowing was done by mouth. Technology has invented tools which manufacture glass vases, bottles, etc.

Butter was made by hand. A machine has been invented which churns vast quantities of milk in a much shorter period of time; this machine is now universally employed.

Dough is kneaded by hand in the little baker's shop; the machine does it in a bread factory.

Light was produced by the mother of the family in the old-fashioned household. She cleaned and filled the lamp, taking care to trim the wick. In the modern home, gas or electricity is supplied from afar by machinery.

Everywhere you look, you see changes in the productive forces in every sector of industry, as well as increasingly rapid transformation and faster-paced evolution. The machine executes operations that were once thought to be impossible for machines.

Along with the productive forces, the relations of production and the mode of production also change. We have already mentioned weaving machinery and how it introduced new relations among the business owners, and between the business owners and the workers. Previously, there were numerous artisans with adjoining little workshops, and proportionally few wage workers. Now there are hundreds of thousands of wage workers and proportionally few factory owners, few entrepreneurs in this industry. The manufacturers conduct themselves in their relations with one another like great lords while they act like Asiatic despots towards the workers. How these relations have changed! All of this, furthermore, was determined by the machine alone.

For it is the machine that has enriched those who could afford to buy one, the machine put them into a position to overcome their competitors, to obtain an enormous amount of capital on credit and, perhaps, to form a trust. And it is the machine, the force of production, which has caused the small business owners to lose their property and has compelled thousands of them to enter the ranks of wage labor.

And what consequences have resulted from the new productive forces employed in the production of butter? The machine, which transforms thousands of liters of milk into butter, was too expensive for the average peasant, who furthermore did not produce enough milk to use it. That is why a hundred peasants join together to buy one, and now they process their milk collectively. The productive force has been modified, but so too have the relations of production, as well as the whole way the product is produced; where formerly one hundred people worked separately, where the wives and children of the peasants made butter under conditions of agricultural exploitation, now one hundred people cooperate to make wage workers labor on behalf of their collective. The peasants, their wives, their children and a certain number of proletarians have entered into new relations of production with each other and with society as a whole.

It used to be the woman of the house who took care of the gas or oil lamp; hundreds of thousands of women were kept busy providing lighting for the home. But if the municipality builds a manufactured gas plant or an electric power station, then the relations of production are modified. It is not a particular human being who produces, but a vast social organism: the municipality. A new type of worker, previously rare, makes its appearance by the thousands: municipal employees, who have a totally different relation to society than the old producers of illumination.

Long ago, wagons were used to transport commodities and mail from one place to another. Technology has invented the locomotive and the telegraph and has thus made it possible for the capitalist State to attract the transport of goods, men, and information. Hundreds of thousands of workers and employees have entered new relations of production. The human masses in the municipality, the State or the Empire, are in a direct relation of production with the collectivity and are much more numerous than the armed hordes of the past.

There is no activity which has not seen technology introduce a new way of production. From top to bottom, from scientific research in chemistry, from the inventor's laboratory to the humblest labor and sewage disposal in a modern big city, technology and work routines are constantly changing. Every activity has been revolutionized, so that inventions are no longer the work of chance or of genius but are the work of people who are trained for the purpose of discovering inventions, and who consciously pursue certain paths towards that end.

One after another, production sectors are transformed or even eliminated. The economic life of a modern capitalist country is like a modern city where new construction replaces whole neighborhoods.

The new technology engenders big capital, and thus also gives rise to the modern banking and credit system which multiplies yet further the powers of big capital.

It gives rise to modern trade, it gives rise to the export of goods and capital, and that is why the seas are covered with fleets and whole regions of the world are subjected to capitalism for the production of minerals and agricultural products.

It gives rise to such huge capitalist interests that only the State is powerful enough to defend them. It therefore gives rise to the modern capitalist State itself, with its militarism, its taste for naval flotillas, its colonialism and imperialism, with its army of functionaries and its bureaucracy.

Is it necessary for us to use such examples to draw the attention of the workers to the fact that the new production relations are also property relations? The number of owners of means of production in the German Empire decreased by 84,000 in industry and 68,000 in agriculture between 1895 and 1907, while the population dramatically increased; on the other hand, the number of men who live from the sale of their labor power increased by three million in industry and 1,660,000 in agriculture. This change, which affected not just production relations but also property relations, was provoked by the new technology, which has smothered small business and has transformed hundreds of thousands of the children of the petit-bourgeoisie and peasantry into wage workers. And what else is the so-called new middle class but a class with new property relations? Functionaries, whose numbers are rapidly increasing, officials, scientists, the intelligentsia, the higher-paid professors, the engineers, chemists, lawyers, doctors, artists, managers, traveling salesmen, the small shopkeepers dependent on big capital, everyone who receives remuneration for services to the bourgeoisie directly or indirectly by way of the State, this new middle class exists in a property relation distinct from that of the old autonomous middle class. And the modern big capitalists who rule the world and world politics with their banks, their syndicates, their trusts and their cartels, exist in property relations vis-à-vis society which are totally different from those of the Florentines, the Venetians, or the Hanseatic, Flemish, Dutch or English traders and industrialists of centuries past.

Production and property relations are therefore not personal, but class relations.

The new technology creates, on the one hand, propertyless people whose numbers are increasing at a faster rate than the general population, who are slowly becoming most of the population, and who receive almost none of the social wealth, as well as a very large number of petit-bourgeois and peasants, employees and practitioners of the most diverse trades, who get very little of the social wealth. On the other hand, however, technology creates a proportionally small number of capitalists who, by way of their political and economic domination, get the greater part by far of the social wealth.

And the surplus they amass each year is once again used to exploit those who have little or nothing, the workers, peasants and petit-bourgeois, and foreign peoples in countries which have not yet undergone capitalist development, so that accumulation takes place, at compound interest, progressively growing, and deprivation is aggravated on the one hand, and a surplus of social wealth comes into being on the other hand.

The constant progress of technology therefore creates not only new relations of production and property, but also new class relations and, in our case, a sharper class divide and more widespread class struggle.

Is it not true that the whole world sees this? It is not hard to see. The classes have turned on each other; the contemporary class struggle is sharper, more extensive, and more profound than it has been for fifty years. With each passing year the abyss has grown wider and deeper and is getting bigger every day. It is absolutely clear that the cause of this is technology.

It is easy to understand the material side of this issue. Does it take many words to explain to the son of a Saxon or Westphalian peasant, who has become a factory worker, that it was technology which made this happen, that it was a result of the new methods of production? That there was no future for him in a small business, that today's competition is too fierce, that too much capital is required, that only a few people can succeed in small business, but that the great majority must labor fruitlessly? Big capital is big technology; who can amass such capital with big technology? The modern worker knows full well that the material situation, bad food, bad housing, and bad clothing for him and his class, are the consequences of the new production relations which have arisen from the old production relations thanks to technology. It is not hard to discern the material existence of all the classes in clearly defined relation to the relations of production and of property and, therefore, to the productive forces. Now no one can point to the expensive clothes, the excellent food, and the luxurious home of the manufacturer as a gift from God, because it is clear that he obtained his well-being and his fortune thanks to exploitation. No one can see "predestination" at work in the downfall of the wholesaler or the speculator because the cause of their downfall must be sought in value or commodity exchange. No one can speak of heaven's wrath when a worker is struck down by unemployment for months, by illness and enduring poverty, because the natural causes, or, more properly speaking, the social causes of all these things, all of which have their roots in the new technologies, are sufficiently well-known, at least by the worker. Nor can one any longer stand for making personal intellectual faculties or individual character responsible for one's prosperity or misfortune, because in the big business, which is replacing everything, millions of people with excellent talents cannot advance.

Society has reached such a level of development that the material causes of our material existence openly reside, for all to see, in society as well as in nature.

Just as we know that the sun is the source of all material life on earth, so too do we know that the labor process and the relations of production are the causes of the way things are in social material life.

If the worker looked calmly and steadily at his material existence, that of his comrades and of the classes above him, he would discover that what has been said above is correct. This would free him from many prejudices and superstitions.

At first sight, the question becomes more difficult when it is a matter of recognizing the relation between material labor, the relations of production and property, and mental existence. The soul, the spirit, the heart, reason; these have been presented to us for a long time, to us and our predecessors, as what is our own, as what is best, as the all-powerful (and even, from time to time, as all that exists)!

Nonetheless . . . when we say: "Social existence determines consciousness," this thesis is, undoubtedly, in its universal significance, a great new truth but, even before Marx and Engels, that which pointed in this direction and paved the way for the higher truth which they discovered, had already been explained, proven and acknowledged.

Does not every educated man believe, does he not know, for example, that before Marx and Engels had clearly proven so much, men's customs, experience, education and environment also shaped them mentally? And our customs—are they not products of society? The men who educate us—have they not been educated themselves by society, and do they not give us a social education? Our experience—is it not social experience? We do not live alone like Robinson Crusoe! Our environment is, then, society first of all; we can only live in nature with our society. All of this is true, and it has also been acknowledged by people who are neither Marxists nor social democrats.

But materialism does not stop there; it summarizes all previous science, but goes deeper by saying: social experience, social customs, education, and environment are themselves determined in turn by social labor and social relations of production. The latter determines all mental existence. Labor is the root of the human mind. The mind is born from that root.

V Social Existence Determines Mental Existence

A. Science, Knowledge, and Learning

Science is an important domain of the mind, although it does not constitute all of it. How can its contents be determined?

The worker must first, while reading this, observe himself. Where does the extent and type of knowledge which fills his mind come from?

He has some knowledge of reading, writing and arithmetic—we are speaking generally, since here we are discussing an ordinary member of the working class who is not in an exceptional situation. In his youth, he may have learned some other things: a little geography, a little history, but remembers nothing of these subjects. Why did he have precisely this miserable education and nothing more?

This is determined by the process of production, with its relations of production. The class of capitalists, which rules in the so-called civilized countries, needs, for its workshops, workers who are not totally ignorant. This is why it introduced elementary schools for the children of proletarians and set the maximum age for receiving this education at 12 to 14 years. The bourgeoisie needed, in the process of production, workers who were neither more ignorant, nor more educated. If they were more ignorant, they would not have been profitable enough, while if they were more educated, they would have been too expensive and too demanding. In the same way that the process of production needs certain machines which run faster and supply more products, it also needs a certain kind of worker, the modern proletarian, unlike the workers of the past. The process of production imposes this need on society; it creates this need as a result of its own nature. In the eighteenth century, for example, there was no need for workers of this kind.

The same thing also took place with the knowledge of the other classes.

Big capitalist industry, communications and agriculture increasingly rely upon the physical and natural sciences. The process of production is a conscious scientific process. The new technology has itself laid the foundations of the modern natural sciences by inventing tools for them and by providing them with the means of communication which bring them material from every country. Production consciously utilizes the forces of nature. As a result, the process of production needs men who understand the natural sciences, mechanics, and chemistry, since only such men can take responsibility for the direction of production and discover new methods and new tools. This is why, because they are social requirements of the process of production, the secondary school and the institution of higher learning are often organized principally with a view towards the study of nature, and they teach those sciences which are necessary for the direction and extension of the process of production.

Knowledge, the sum of all the particular knowledge of all these mechanics, shipbuilders, engineers, agronomists, chemists, mathematicians, and science teachers, is therefore determined by the process of production.

We shall draw a second example from these same social classes. The activity of lawyers, professors of law and economics, judges, notaries, etc., does it not presuppose a certain property law, that is, as we have seen above, certain relations of production? The notaries, lawyers, etc., are these not people who are needed by capitalist society for the preservation and protection of the rights of property? Therefore, is it not true that their way of thinking is inspired by the bourgeois class, and their thought has its source in the process of production which has engendered these classes?

The nobility, the bureaucracy, the parliament—do they not presuppose property or class interests based on relations of production, interests which must by protected at home against the other classes and overseas against other peoples? Is the government not the central committee of the bourgeoisie which defends their property and interests? The government itself, as well as the knowledge and special techniques which it possesses for that purpose, are born from social needs, from the needs of the process of production and property. The knowledge of its members is used for the preservation of the existing relations of production and property.

And what is the role of the clergy, of the minister and the priest? If they are reactionaries, they officially serve—with their demand that one must unconditionally submit to the dogmas of the Church and to certain moral precepts—to uphold the old society. This is what their knowledge is used for, this is why they were educated in institutions of higher learning; there is a social need, a class need, for people who preach such things. If they are progressives, they proclaim the rule of God over the world, the rule of the spirit over matter, and thus help the bourgeoisie—who have educated them for this purpose—to preserve their rule over labor.

The system of production and property required the cultivation of a certain kind of priest, judge, physicist, and technician. It produced them and, through social necessity, the protagonists and representatives of these social roles have continuously been making their appearance en masse in society. The individual imagines that he freely chooses one of the professions and that the conceptions nourished in them "are the determinant characteristic causes and the point of departure for his activity". In reality these conceptions and his choice, first of all, are determined by the process of production.

"In the social production of their lives," Marx says, "men enter into necessary and determined relations, independent of their wills, relations of production." This is certainly true. These relations are necessary and independent of our will. They were already present before we were born. We must necessarily enter into these relations; society, with its process of production, with its classes and needs, has us in its power.

And all these kinds of professions require a certain amount and a certain type of knowledge to fulfill their functions in society. It is therefore clear that, like their functions themselves, the various kinds of knowledge required by society are determined by the social process of production.

In this first discussion we have addressed the issue of knowledge, which plays an important role in society and thus, in our doctrine, which is the true image of society, a role which we must therefore mention again and again. It is a question of necessity.

Necessity, however, is something mental, it is felt, perceived and thought, in the soul, in the heart, in the spirit and in the brain of man.

With this argument, the opponents of social democracy forge a weapon against us.

They say that if the institutions of the process of production are engendered by man's need, then the cause of this need is, first of all, spiritual and not material social.

This objection is easy to refute. Where, after all, do needs come from? Are they born from free will, are they based on opinion? Are they the independent results of the spirit? No, needs originate in man's corporeal nature. Above all, if the needs of food, clothing and shelter are not met, men would perish miserably. The activity of procuring food, clothing, and shelter, for the production and reproduction of life, is the purpose of the process of production; when we speak of production, we must always include the production of those articles which men need in order to live.

But if man in general has need of food, clothing and shelter, each mode of production implies its own particular needs. Such needs are always rooted in the process of production. Today, the production of our vital necessities is only possible by way of big industry, under the protection of State power; it therefore requires a highly developed science; it requires people who understand science. The student, for example, needs knowledge of mechanics, law, theology, and political science; but who provided him with these needs? Society, his society, with its particular process of production, which, without such knowledge, could neither exist nor produce his means of subsistence. In a different form of society, he might not have desired these fields of knowledge and might have aspired to study completely different subjects.

The worker also feels the need for knowledge, that is, for knowledge of society, for the kind of knowledge we are attempting to give him at this very moment—a knowledge of a completely different kind than that which is given him in the school of the ruling class—but where does this need come from? From the process of production. For the latter transforms the worker into a member of a class which numbers in the millions, which must fight and can attain victory. If this were not so, the worker would not seek such knowledge. In the eighteenth century, he did not yet seek it because the relations of production were of another kind during that era and did not provoke this need in him.

It is therefore only an illusion to think that it is the need for knowledge, the spiritual sensation of the soul, which leads us. If we reflect deeply, we see that this need is inspired within us by social-material relations.

This is true not only in the case of the "higher" spiritual need for knowledge but is also true of much "lower" things; material needs are also often determined by technology, by the relations of production and of property.

The worker needs, for example, food like any other man, but does he need margarine, does he need ersatz food, or substitutes for his clothing, his comfort, and his adornment? Honestly, no. It must instead be said that man, by his nature, desires food which invigorates him and good clothing to adorn him. But if the system of production and of property needed cheap food for the workers, it experienced the need to give rise to mass-produced articles; it produced them, and only in this way and only for this reason has the need for these cheap, mass-produced, low-quality products arisen.

Thus, no one needs, in and of itself, a production process capable of producing 100,000 pieces per hour or one that runs at the speed of one hundred kilometers per hour; only the producer who is under the pressure of competition needs it as a consequence of the system of production; the latter produces the machines which attain such speeds and such levels of productivity, and only in this way and for this reason is this need felt by all of society's individuals.

We could thus provide hundreds of examples. The reader will easily find them by just looking around.

"Is the system of needs based on opinion, or on the complete organization of production? In most cases, needs are born from production or from a general situation based on production. World trade almost exclusively revolves around the needs of production rather than individual consumption." And in this manner knowledge, too, is born from the needs of production.

The Second Objection

But—say our opponents—there is a general desire for knowledge common to all men! The desire for any particular kind of knowledge might be temporary, but the general desire for knowledge is eternal.

Not at all. There are people who have absolutely no desire for knowledge, who are perfectly satisfied with the little passed on to them by their ancestors in the way of science.

In a lush tropical region where nature provides the inhabitants with all they need, the latter are content when they can plant their palm trees and when they know how to build a hut with branches and leaves, and when they know how to do a few other things, of great antiquity, which have been transmitted to them from the past. In countries with fertile soil and small-scale agriculture, the inhabitants can remain in the same situation for centuries. They do not seek new knowledge because the relations of production do not require this of them.

A convincing example—which we have not yet mentioned—is provided by those peoples who practice agriculture in the valleys of large rivers which flood periodically: they needed an astronomical calendar and were therefore obliged to study the celestial bodies.

Such were the inhabitants of Egypt, Mesopotamia, and China, who arrived at astronomy on account of the Nile, the Euphrates and the Yellow River. Other people, who did not experience the need for this knowledge, did not become acquainted with it.

It is, then, the relations of production which drive knowledge, and which determine the quantity and the quality of this knowledge.

To verify this truth, the worker only needs to take a look around him once again. Who are the active workers, the ones with a thirst for learning, the ones who are full of the desire for social development? The ones who can understand the role of the proletariat in the context of the process of production, that is, the workers in cities and big industry. Technology, the machine itself, tells them that a socialist society is possible; the vast process of production which they have before their eyes teaches them that the old relations of productions are too narrow for the forces of the machine. New relations must come; as you are equal in terms of rights, you must yourselves take possession of the means of production: these are the words that are shouted in their ears by the modern city. And thanks to these words of the process of production, a desire for knowledge is born in the workers of the cities which is much stronger than that of the rural worker, who does not yet see so much of the new forces of production.

Observation

On the basis of the example of the tropical regions, where the process of production does not spur the search for knowledge, and of the example of the great river valleys, where the desire for knowledge was aroused, the attentive reader sees that historical materialism does not recognize the process of production as the sole cause of this development. Geographical factors have great importance in historical materialism. Thus, and to take one last important example, the process of production would never have developed so vigorously and rapidly in Europe if the latter had a tropical climate and if the soil had provided abundant harvests almost without labor. It is precisely Europe's temperate climate and its relatively poor soil which obliged its people to work harder and, for that very reason, to acquire an understanding of nature.

Thus, the reproach that the process of production is for the social democrats the only independent motor force is unfounded. Besides the climate and the natural qualities of a country, besides the influences of the atmosphere and the soil, we shall learn to recognize still other motor forces in the course of our argument.

There is a domain of science which must be discussed in more detail. That is the domain of technological inventions.

We said: the relations of production rest upon technology. Do we not also thereby admit that the relations of production rest upon the mind?

Of course, we do. Technology is the invention and the conscious utilization of tools by thinking man, and when the defenders of historical materialism say that all of society rests upon technology, they are also simultaneously saying that all of society rests upon material and mental labor.

But does this not contradict what we said? Does this not thus convert the mind once again into the leading motor force of social evolution?

If the mind produces technology and technology produces society, then the mind is undoubtedly the first creator.

Let us take an even closer look at this question.

Historical materialism by no means denies that the mind is part of technology. Men are thinking beings. The relations of production, the relations of property, are relations between men; it is within these relations that they act and think. Technology and the relations of property and production are just as mental as they are material. This is not the object of our dispute.

We only deny the autonomous, arbitrary, spontaneous, supernatural, and incomprehensible nature of the mind and its activity. We say: if the mind discovers a new science, or a new technology, it does not do so of its own volition but as the result of an impulse or a need of society.

In other times, most technological inventions were made by men who were themselves involved in the process of production. It was their desire to improve the labor process and to make it more efficient to make more wealth for themselves or to enrich the whole world!

Whatever the nature of society, whether large or small, nomadic horde or tribe, feudal or capitalist, this desire was social; it was engendered by an economic need. In societies where property was held in common, it was the social desire to do something for the community; in class societies with private property, it was the social desire to do something for the social individual, for the private owner or for the class of private masters.

There is nothing surprising about this. Since man is a social being and man's labor is social, the desire to improve labor is not something which results from the mind of the individual, but something which derives from his social relations. The desire for an improved technology, for inventions, is a social desire; it is born from social needs.

This is what the defenders of historical materialism say: they deny the independence, the arbitrariness, the preeminence of the mind; they say that existing social need obliges the mind to follow a particular road and that this need is also engendered by specific material relations of production. Therefore, they also deny the absolute mastery of the mind.

This relation between technology and science is so important that we are well advised to pause and give it more thorough consideration.

We shall provide a few detailed examples.

Let us consider a weaver of the Middle Ages. The job done by the weaver is generally sufficient for social needs. Trade, circulation, and the foreign market have not yet developed to the point where large-scale productive forces are necessary. The need for them is not yet felt. However, the especially wise weaver cannot neglect his tools since he knows that a more convenient and efficient manner of production would benefit him personally. He invents a small improvement and implements it. Within his circle, this improvement is noted and imitated. And that is as far as it goes. It is a small change in the process of production which barely signifies a step forward and which might be the only such change for decades or centuries. It was the result of an individual's need.

Let us suppose, however, that circulation and trade have made great progress (as in the fifteenth, sixteenth and seventeenth centuries, for example), that the foreign market has seen extraordinary growth, and that colonies have been founded which generate a demand for manufactured goods from their home countries; then, the social need and desire for improved technology, and for greater labor productivity, become generalized;

then, it is not one man who ponders the subject of technological improvements, but one hundred men who do so; then a new instrument is born as the result of numerous, rapidly-accumulating changes.

Let us consider one of the inventors of the steam engine, Papin, for example.

In many men there is a special talent and love for technology; this is a legacy of millions of years of human evolution; in some men, when the relations of production contribute their stimulus, this love and this talent are most conspicuous. The society in which they live now has a developed technology; they study an improvement which could enhance social productivity. Their social reflection, oriented by this purpose, is devoted to the power of pressurized steam. They imagine a new apparatus based on the old instruments powered by men, animals, water, or wind. Their social feelings are so overwhelming, their happiness and their desire to produce something of this sort are so strong, that they sacrifice their time, their health and their wealth to perfect it and to make it accepted.

The generalized need, however, still does not exist; this particular step forward for technology is so big that the price to develop it is too high. The invention is not introduced, the experiments must be stopped and fall into oblivion. The inventor often goes to his grave a ruined man. He certainly did discern a social need, but society had not yet experienced this need, or, in any case, it did not feel it sufficiently; the inventor arrived too soon.

Now let us consider an inventor of our time, Edison. He is a technician; his life consists solely of thinking about technology. But he is not a man born before his time who thinks of what is not yet possible. Society, or in any case the owning classes, wants the same thing he does. For the capitalists, improved technology means a colossal increase in profit. Every invention which makes cheaper and faster production possible is immediately adopted. This increases the power of labor and allows the latter to pose its own problems, which no longer depend on chance but on its own will.

An Edison's desire for invention is a social desire, his love of technology is a love engendered in and by society, a social love;

the basis upon which he labors is also social; that he is successful and can consciously posit his object in advance, is due to society.

In our days it often happens that new machines are invented but cannot be introduced because they are too expensive. In agriculture, for example, there are excellent machines which, for the most part, remain utterly unutilized or are only used sparingly. The relations of production are still too limited for these new forces. Thus, if an invention arises as the consequence of a social need felt by an individual on the basis of an already-existing technology, nonetheless only those inventions which society needs in practice, and which can be introduced in its specific relations will be adopted. Consequently, both the birth and the development of the tool are of a social nature. Their roots are not to be found in the mind of the individual but in society.

In conclusion, here is an example drawn from the era when man was only just beginning to fabricate his first tools. It is from Kautsky's book, Ethics and the Materialist Conception of History. There we read (p. 83):

"Ever since primitive man possessed the spear; he could herd much larger animals. If his food had hitherto consisted for the most part of fruits and insects, as well as birds' eggs and chicks, now he could also kill much larger animals, and henceforth meat became a more important part of his diet. But most animals live on the ground rather than in the trees; therefore, the hunt descended from its airy regions to an earth-bound domain. Even more: the animals which could be hunted, the ruminants, are only rarely found in the virgin forest; they prefer the vast plains of the savannahs. The more of a hunter man became, the more he could leave the virgin tropical forest where prehistoric man was hidden away."

"This description is, as has been pointed out, based purely on suppositions. The course of evolution could just as well have been otherwise. Just as the inventions of the tool and the weapon could have been capable of impelling man to leave the virgin forest to migrate to the open savannah with its scattered woodlands, it could also have been the case that some other cause led man to leave his original abode and thereby presented him with the occasion to invent weapons and tools. Let us assume, for example, that man's population had increased beyond his ability to feed himself . . . or that a drought had thinned out the virgin forests, and that this led to the appearance of more prairies among the forestlands. In any event prehistoric man was compelled to renounce his sylvan ways and move closer to the ground; then he had to seek more animal food and could no longer feed himself on a predominantly fruit-based diet. The new way of life gave him the chance to make more frequent use of rocks and sticks and thus brought him closer to the invention of the first tools and the first weapons."

"Whatever course of evolution one presupposes, the first or the second—and both could have taken place independently in different locations—one may clearly deduce from each the strict interaction which exists between new means of production and new ways of life, new needs. Each of these factors engenders the other by objective necessity; each is transformed by necessity into the cause of changes which in turn contain new changes within them. Thus, every invention produces inevitable effects which give rise to other inventions and therefore to new needs and new ways of life as well, which in turn stimulate new inventions, etc., a chain of infinite development which becomes always more varied and rapid as it advances and with which the possibility and the likelihood of new inventions increases."

Kautsky goes on to tell how man, once he arrived on the grassy plains, devoted himself to agriculture, to the construction of dwellings, to the use of fire and to the breeding of cattle, and how, later, "man's whole life, his needs, his dwelling-places, his means of subsistence, were changed and how an invention had in the end led to many more after it, once it had been discovered, once the fabrication of the spear or some other device was achieved".

Observation

The invention of new technology, upon which, as we have seen, science rests, takes place through social desire and social need which find their expression in the individual, and can only totally succeed when this need is felt by all of society. Until that moment, however, the mind of the inventor cannot foresee in most cases the invention's possible consequences.

Did the inventors of the steam engine or even the inventors of the powerful technologies of our time foresee that the class struggle between labor and capital would become more rigorous and aggravated as a result of their inventions? Do our inventors see that the socialist society must be born from their inventions? All men, even the most brilliant, have to this day been blind to society's future. They were obliged to act within the framework of social needs. Under capitalism, men became aware of these needs, although only vaguely, but they did not know where the satisfaction of these needs would lead society. They lived in the realm of necessity.

Only in socialist society, when the means of production are collective property, when they are consciously utilized and controlled, only then will man be aware of not only the social forces and needs which oblige him to act, but also the goal towards which his activity leads and the consequences which flow from his activity. Each technological improvement will have consequently greater happiness, and more freedom for mental and physical development. No invention will give birth to unforeseen horrible setbacks; all of them will grant individuals the freedom for development towards improvement and will thus continuously improve the conditions for all men's happiness.

In all actuality, the productive forces, the material relations of production, are pushing us towards socialism and, within the socialist society as well, we will depend upon the productive forces, on the socialist mode of production. Since social existence will always have precedence over the mind, we shall never be free. But if we no longer blindly and passively endure this condition, if we are no longer dragged along by the explosive movement of technology like poor isolated "atoms", if we consciously produce as a single whole, if we foresee the consequences of our social actions, then we will be free, in comparison with today's conditions, then we will have passed from the dark realm of blind fate to the magnificent light of freedom. Nor shall we then enjoy absolute freedom, which exists only in the brains of the anarchists and the priests or mystical liberals; we shall be connected to the productive forces at our disposal. But we will be capable of using them in accordance with our common will, in accordance with our collective benefit. And that is all we are demanding.

Naturally, once a science has been called into existence by a social need, it can continue to develop, regardless of its stage of development, without any direct connection to social need. Although the beginnings of astronomy resulted from a social need, it later continued to develop outside of any direct connection to the needs of the life of society. Nonetheless, the relation between a science which has become autonomous, technology and need, must constantly be uncovered if we are not to be limited to just the branches or the blossoms but see the roots of science.

C. Law

Law is about what is mine and what is yours. Law is the general concept of a society to which you, I and the other person belong. If the productive forces and the relations of production are stable, these ideas of property will not change. But if the former begins to waiver, the latter will become unstable as well. This is not surprising. For the relations of production are at the same time property relations, as we clearly demonstrated above.

We shall provide a few important examples, with which everyone is familiar, drawn from our own times, to illustrate these changes.

Not so long ago, in a big city like Amsterdam, it was generally accepted that the provision of lighting and water, as well as transportation, was an occasion for private individuals to make money; gas works, the water supply and streetcars had to be the property of private individuals. Things are different now. Today it is generally acknowledged that these activities, and many other sectors of industry, should be municipally owned. This is a great transformation in the conception of law, in the domain of the mind, which expresses an opinion, a conviction or a prejudice concerning what is mine and what is yours.

It is not hard to show that it came directly from a change in the productive forces. When Holland began to suffer from the influence of big industry and world trade, the situation of the middle class and the working class deteriorated. Their situation became even worse after 1870. These classes of the population reflected upon the question of how to remedy their misery. This led to the birth of a middle-class party which was joined by the workers. When this party took power, it introduced municipal ownership so that its members would no longer be bled by the private companies which exploited the gas works, the water system, and streetcars.

The new economic relation between big capital, on the one side, and the small businessmen and craftsmen, on the other, which is, basically, the relation between the big machine and the small tool-bench, created for one part of society, for certain classes, a new condition of need. The need for new relations of production was born, thanks to which the new productive forces were to inflict fewer devastating results. The classes which suffered the effects of these new productive forces managed to take power and introduced new property relations.

This is a relatively minor example. Even though the municipal enterprise (and even the national enterprise) is a completely different form of property compared to the private business owned by one or more capitalists, everyone knows that today's municipality or State is capitalist and that the benefits of the municipal enterprise or State property cannot be very significant for the ordinary man. But however much the humble folk are conned, fleeced or shaken down by the State as well as by the municipality, they will not be bled quite as shamelessly as they were by the owners of private utilities.

The example of our own movement is of much greater significance and of much greater scope.

Socialism wants to transform the means of production into collective property. There are now millions of socialists where there were practically none a few decades ago. How has such a vast revolution in thought, in the consciousness of so many men, taken place? How has their conception of law been transformed?

Here, the answer is much clearer than in the case of the first example.

Big industry has made it plain to millions of proletarians that, if private property in the means of production lasts, they will never have property or well-being. But if private property is transformed into common property, then the road to well-being is open to them. This is why they became socialists.

In addition, crises and overproduction, as well as, more recently, the trusts, with their competition which devours everything and their restriction of production—all these factors which derive directly from the contemporary private ownership of the means of production—have had such an awful effect on the middle classes that even among the latter many consider collective property as the only way to save themselves from poverty, and they became socialists.

With socialism, the direct relation between the change in the productive forces and relations of production, and the change in thought, is evident.

Is it a god which has put socialism into our heads? Is it a mystical spark, a holy spirit? A light which god has shown us, as many Christian socialists would have us believe?

Is it our own free mind which has produced for us this magnificent thought due to the excellence of the mind? Is it our own especially elevated virtue, a secret force within us, the categorical imperative of Kant?

Or is the devil that has instilled in us the desire for collective property? This is what other Christians declare.

None of the above. It is poverty, social misery.

This poverty comes from the fact that the new productive forces, within the straitjacket of the old property relations of the small business of past times, wreak devastation among the workers and the petit bourgeois. The solution of socialism arises on its own because all the workers and many petit bourgeois can sense and understand that this devastation would come to an end if they were to collectively own the means of production. Labor is already certainly collective. The fact that their difficulties could be resolved thanks to common ownership is therefore obvious.

Nor can it be said that socialism was contemplated over the course of centuries past and that therefore socialism cannot be an emanation of today's dominant productive forces, but that the principle of the equality of all men is an eternal ideal which men have dreamed about in every era.

Socialism as conceived by the first Christians was as unlike the socialism sought by today's working class as the productive forces and class relations of that epoch are unlike today's productive forces and class relations. The first Christians wanted a common consumption, the rich were supposed to share their surplus of means of consumption with the poor. It was not the soil, the land and the means of labor which were to be held in common, but the products. It was, then, basically a socialism of beggars; the poor, thanks to the goodness of the rich, were supposed to share the products with the latter.

Likewise, Jesus himself never preached anything else, that is, that the rich should give up their wealth. The rich were supposed to love the poor as brothers and the poor were to love the rich in the same way.

Social democracy, on the other hand, teaches that those who possess nothing must fight the owners and seize from them the means of production through political power; it does not want to possess the products in a collective manner—to the contrary, what each receives in the way of products, of objects of consumption, will be for him alone, he need not share it—but it most certainly does want to collectively possess the means of production.

The relations of production of the first centuries of Christianity could not have given rise to our social democratic conceptions, any more than our productive forces can lead us to the Christian ideal. When the productive forces were still so minimal, so fragmented and dispersed in such a way that a greater community could not control them, the only solution to poverty was philanthropy, as miserable and insufficient as it was, since it only alleviated an insignificant part of that poverty. In an era where labor is becoming increasingly social, social ownership is the only means to confront poverty, but now it is also a sufficient means.

Another significant example is provided by criminal law. Here, too, a revolution has taken place in the minds of many men: socialist workers no longer believe in the personal fault of the criminal. They believe that the causes of crime are social rather than personal.

How did they arrive at this new opinion, which neither liberal nor clerical Christianity could discover?

It was possible thanks to the struggle against capitalism which, as we saw above, rests upon the process of production. Socialist authors were led by the struggle, by their critique of the existing social order, to look for the causes of crime, and they discovered that the causes of crime are rooted in society. It was the process of production and the class struggle which necessarily led them to this understanding.

This awareness is slowly penetrating the minds of socialistically educated workers.

We cannot provide further examples for reasons of space, but this example once again reveals the revolution which has taken place in the world of thought because of the change in the relations of production. And how different things are today! It was not so long ago that the world believed in sin, in personal culpability, in free will, in the vengeance of God and men, in punishment; now, socialists—but only socialists—see that, when "the anti-social roots of crime are annihilated, along with capitalist society, and when every person is provided with the social space for his essential life expression", then social crime will disappear.

Observation

At this point, after examining these examples of changes in thinking about law and property, we now very clearly discern for the first time a law of the evolution of human thought that has not yet been subjected to our closest scrutiny.

We have already seen enough concerning the question of why evolution in thought is engendered by the productive forces, which are its wellsprings and causes. Now, we will see how this takes place. Evolution in thought takes place in struggle, in the class struggle. This can be illustrated quite clearly with the same examples of municipal utilities and the socialist conception of property and law which we discussed above.

Big industry made the situation of the petit-bourgeois and the workers extremely difficult. Monopolies controlling the supply of gas and water, taken for granted for years, became increasingly unendurable as big industry continued to expand. The workers and the petit bourgeois viewed the monopolies as their enemies, and to free themselves from the control of the latter became a vital necessity. The following thought took shape in their minds: what would be just, just to the highest degree, would be for the municipality to control this kind of activity. We, the laboring classes, must fight these parasites. The parasites, on the other hand, thought it was our right to own these utilities; as a class we will lose all our profits if we allow one profitable business after another to be taken from us. We must fight the laboring classes. It is, then, in the struggle where a new conception of law has evolved. The development of the new productive forces has produced a new class struggle, and this struggle has expanded the new legal consciousness.

And the proletariat, which had the feeling that it was intellectually, morally, and physically dying at the hands of big industry, recognized the capitalists as its enemies. First, it thought we, the workers in this factory, are deprived, we are dying, and our capitalist is our enemy; it is unjust that he receives all the profits and we get nothing. We must fight him. Later, the proletariat of a whole city, or of a particular trade, thought the same thing. And then the proletariat of an entire country and of the whole world. All of them thought we, as a class, must fight the class of capitalists. It would be right for all the means of production to be in our hands. We shall struggle for our rights.

The capitalists, however, thought precisely the contrary, first individually, then all of them together, in an organized way and as a State. It is right for us to keep what belongs to us. We shall crush these revolutionary ideas. We shall struggle together as a class for our rights.

And the more that technology developed, the more that the productive forces and wealth in the hands of the capitalists constantly grew, the deeper, the more widespread and the less endurable became the poverty among a continuously growing proletariat; and the more that the owners recognized the necessity of preserving their greater wealth, the greater was the necessity asserted by those who owned nothing of seizing the means of production. So also, to the same degree the struggle between the two classes has grown sharper and for that same reason so has the power of their ideas concerning what is right and what is wrong become more well-defined.

With this example we see quite clearly that the conceptions of what is right and what is wrong evolve in the class struggle and as a result of the class struggle, and that a class could slowly come to consider something to be wrong which previously seemed right, and that it could also, with the growth of class interests, feel this new sense of what is right and wrong with an increasing passion.

The material struggle for the means of production is simultaneously a spiritual struggle concerning what is right and wrong. The wrong is the mental mirror-image of the right.

Second Observation

It will not of course be necessary to show here that, in this spiritual and material struggle, the victorious class will be the one which, in the end, due to the development of the process of production, will be transformed into the most powerful class, the class with the greatest spiritual power and the greater truth, the class which, as a result of the needs brought about by its situation, will be called upon to resolve the contradictions between the new productive forces and the old relations of production. We shall return to this topic at the end of our treatise. At this time, however, we must set forth another observation which will invalidate an objection of our adversaries.

There are members of the owning classes who pass over to the side of those who have nothing. Does this not prove that it is not social existence which determines thought, but that maybe something eminently spiritual, something mysteriously ethical, is what determines our social behavior?

An individual who passes from the capitalist camp to the proletarian camp could do so for two kinds of reasons, reasons which could also be at work simultaneously. Perhaps he has come to understand that the future belongs to the proletariat. But no one can deny that it is the process of production, i.e., the economic relations, which provided him with this understanding and therefore that it is not in the "freedom" of the mind that one must seek the motive for his action, but in social existence. Or this act could be rooted in sentimental reasons, since, for example, this individual prefers to stand alongside the weak rather than the oppressors. During our discussion of social morality we shall prove that, in this case as well, the determinant sentiments are based on the socio-economic life of men rather than something mysterious, supernatural or absolutely spiritual.

D. Politics

If the socialist conceptions of property and crime provide clear examples of how the productive forces influence thought, how the class struggle arises and how it must be resolved, in politics we encounter examples that are yet more clear.

And in this connection, we must also refer to the example of what the socialists think, since it is in their heads that the new productive forces are most vigorously at work.

The new productive forces also powerfully influence the minds of the industrialist, the financier, the wholesaler, the shipbuilder, etc. They think of enormous enterprises, huge profits, the formation of cartels, foreign and colonial markets, the creation of a national navy and a powerful army, in order to increase their influence, their wealth and their power. But regardless of the scale of their thought compared to that of the capitalists and ruling classes of past centuries, the type of thinking they engage in is the same.

The middle classes also think differently than the middle classes of the past. The growth of the productive forces has pushed them in a dangerous direction, into a position where they could fall into the ranks of the proletariat. How to escape this fate—by means of credit, by State aid, through trade unions—this is what they reflect upon, totally unlike their parents. In their minds, things now seem very different from the way they were in the eighteenth century, for example. Their thought, however, moves in the same old direction: profit, profit, and more private profit!

The mind of the non-socialist worker is also full of feelings quite distinct from those experienced by his counterparts of the first half of the nineteenth century, for example. Higher wages, shorter working hours, State aid, a higher standard of living—this is what he thinks about; it is like a beehive, like a millwheel in these non-socialist Christian organizations. This humming and grinding always resounds with the same themes: organization, a higher standard of living. But these men are still treading the old paths; they want to obtain greater benefits from capital, from private property—on the terrain of private property.

Among the socialists, on the other hand, something different is coming to life, something completely new, something which never existed in the world in this form. Even though they stand on the terrain of private property, they want to abolish private property; even though they are living in a capitalist State, they want to overthrow the capitalist State. Born and raised in the shell of capitalism, their thoughts are of eliminating this shell; their thoughts are of transforming their thoughts into other thoughts. The working class wants to destroy the source of its existence, capital, and private property in the means of production. This effect of the productive forces is here completely unlike the effect it has on the other classes, it is much more important, much more profound, and much more radical; and for this reason, socialist thought is the best example of the influence of technology on the mind.

Politics is also where the relation between social existence and thought is especially clearly illuminated, because politics contains the will, desire, hope, thought, and intrigues within the State, the whole life of all classes in the modern State, because the citizen, who has political rights in our State, must reflect upon society as a whole as well as its parts, and because he is therefore concerned with literally the entirety of mental life as a result of society's changes.

What is the most important, the most ubiquitous political issue of our time, the one which could therefore best serve us as an example?

The social question, the question of the struggle between labor and capital.

The question itself arose as a result of capital, that is, due to the development of the productive forces.

And by focusing on the way men think about this question, one can get a better idea of how technological development constrains them to change their way of thinking.

Sixty years ago, for example, how many people would have thought of establishing a maximum legal working day for the proletarians, or of laws protecting women and children, or even a workmen's compensation disability fund? They were few and far between and those who did contemplate such things had received news concerning such labor protection laws from highly developed capitalist countries. It is most likely that no one even considered such things one hundred years ago.

How did this noble idea, that is, that the proletariat should be protected by society, get into people's heads?

It is hardly likely that Christian feeling inspired this idea, because prior to the mental transformation which led to its adoption, thousands and thousands of workers died from overwork, illness, poverty and accidents, thousands upon thousands have grown old in poverty. There were, however, plenty of Christians back then. The fact that no one thought of State aid in other times therefore must have some other cause.

And that cause is not hard to discover. In other times, the proletariat was not yet strong and could not compel the owners to do more than provide private alms and a little public assistance.

The fact that, in those days, the proletariat was not yet strong was due to the process of production, which had not yet organized the workers. They were already numerous enough, but they were dispersed into small enterprises and this is why they were only capable of mobilizing small forces.

But when they were constrained by the process of production to work by the hundreds in factories and workshops, they began to become conscious of their power and of how to organize for the struggle, just as they had been organized for labor. And this struggle, which was born of the process of production, this obvious phenomenon, led the different classes of society to think, and produced a mental revolution.

This took place first, naturally, in England and France, where the new process of production first made its appearance. We shall not pause here to consider these foreign examples; we only wish to show that it was in those countries where, under the influence of the new relations, the utopian socialism of Saint-Simon, Fourier and Robert Owen was born, and where Friedrich Engels, thanks to his knowledge of English production relations, and Karl Marx, thanks to his study of French and English politics, conceived social democratic theory.

But even in Germany one can see the truth of what we have to say about politics.

The workers emerged from the Revolution of 1848 empty handed. The triune Prussian voting system of Estates(1) left them without any political influence. No laws protected them from the awful consequences of increasing capitalist exploitation.

But at the beginning of the 1860s, the workers began to organize. Rebuffed by the bourgeoisie, they founded, under Lassalle's leadership, the General Association of German Workers (Allgemeine Deutsche Arbeiterverein--the ADAV), which assumed the leadership of the struggle for equal universal suffrage. The Junker ruling class took note of this; conservative spokesmen made speeches about the supreme mission of the State to protect the oppressed.

The ADAV's propaganda spread throughout the country. Bismarck introduced universal suffrage, which he had promised before the war against Austria, first in the Confederation of North German States (2) and then in the newly formed German Empire.

Bebel, Liebknecht, and Schweitzer, who were rapidly becoming the spokesmen of the proletariat, were elected to the Reichstag. Trade unions were formed. The number of socialist votes increased with each election. The two fractions of German social democracy merged at Gotha. Due to the growing power of socialism, the ruling class felt increasingly worried, and then anxious. Bismarck tried to squelch the movement with the anti-socialist law.

But the working class could only be vanquished by force. The elections of 1881 demonstrated the law's ineffectiveness. Something had to be done to contain the spread of dissent. A speech by the emperor announced, "a positive improvement in the well-being of the workers". A hastily improvised law concerning paid sick leave, proposed before the Reichstag in 1882, was enacted in 1884.

Despite the anti-socialist law, the socialist movement made great progress. In the elections of 1884, 1887 and 1890, the socialist vote rose from 550,000 to 760,000, then to 1,400,000. The anti-socialist law was jettisoned; Bismarck was dismissed. The legislation proposed in February 1890 promised protection for labor and legal equality of rights for the workers.

What a gigantic reversal in thought! In an entire country, in all classes of the population! Everyone took a stand on the social question, that is, on the class struggle!

And it is obvious that this is related to technological development! Statistics show us that industry developed rapidly in the early 1860s and 1870s, as well as at the end of the 1880s, precisely the years when socialism experienced its fastest rate of growth. One could plot an almost identical graph for the growth of each of the following phenomena: increasing production; the growing army of combatants; and the changing political opinions of the ruling classes. The growth of each one of these factors corresponds to the others; the class struggle obviously derives from technological development.

And how clearly the particular character of this development comes to the fore: struggle. The Emperor and the Chancellor, the ministers and politicians did not arrive at their new ideas by way of Christian sentiment, nor did they do so by way of free will, or the spontaneous and arbitrary operation of reason or under the influence of a spirit from one or another mystical era. It was the workers themselves, upon the basis of their labor, who, through their organization, their propaganda, their struggle, compelled the bourgeoisie to change the contents of their minds.

Here one can disregard all mysticism. The real relations stand out as openly before our eyes as the movements of the planets in our solar system.

The evolution of the minds of the workers originated in technology, and the evolution of the minds of the owning classes derived from the effect exercised upon them by the ideas of the workers, transformed into actions.

This is even more evident regarding later developments. The workers did not allow themselves to be led astray by government promises and voted in even greater numbers for social democracy. Those in power understood that more significant reforms than those they were willing to concede would be necessary to seduce such a class-conscious working class. The pace of social reform slowed appreciably. The power of the proletariat had become too formidable.

During the nineteenth century, the trade unions had become powerful organizations which wrested many reforms from the capitalists. The owning classes once again considered violent repression; proposals for a coup d'état and prisons were brought up, but no one dared to carry them out.

The organization, the class consciousness, the understanding, and the power of the workers has become so great that the ruling classes despair just as much at the prospect of trapping them with reforms as of oppressing them with force. They are devoting themselves to reinforcing the instruments of their power for the purpose of preparing for the struggle for power. Nowhere has the ruling class, armed to the teeth, presented such a mean visage as in Germany. The reason? It was in Germany, like nowhere else in Europe, where big industry underwent the most precipitous growth in the last few decades, amassed the greatest wealth, and most vigorously developed its technology.

At the risk of generating boredom with too many details, we shall pause to examine these questions a little more closely; it is very much in the workers' interest to have a profound grasp of them.

Up to this point we have put all the owning classes in the same bag, as if they constituted a single mass in opposition to the proletariat. There are, however, important differences among them, and the development of technology does not have the same effect on all these classes. It is therefore necessary to address these differences.

The material situations and political opinions of the various classes are affected quite variously by technological development. Let us take, for example, militarism and imperialism, on the one hand, and social legislation, on the other.

Intense international competition compels the big capitalists of all countries to support colonialism. When a State already has colonial possessions, that State's capitalists can then obtain much more wealth in those possessions than in the colonies of other countries. They penetrate their own countries' colonies much more easily right from the start; it is their State which pushes them forward, which helps them and gives them the best protection. A colony is primarily the object of exploitation by its own metropolis. Labor power is cheap in the colony, violence and intimidation are authorized, and colonial profits are often enormous. Surplus capital in the metropolis can be profitably invested in the colony. This is why, for example, the big German capitalists, who gaze with envy upon the gigantic profits which foreign capitalists are extracting from their colonies, push for the greatest expansion of their own country's colonial power.

To achieve this, however, military equipment is required, especially the construction of a navy; not just for the subjection of the colonies themselves, but above all to oppose the other colonial powers which are pursuing the same goal. This is why the big capitalists are demanding millions for the army and the navy.

But the army has yet another purpose. It has the duty of protecting the owners against the working class which is rising in a threatening manner. When the workers, the majority of the population, are cohesively organized and rebelling against the existing order, how else could a ruling minority stay in power except by means of a well-equipped, highly disciplined army, one which blindly obeys its superiors' orders due to its training and fear of barbaric punishments? Fear of the socialist proletariat leads to the bourgeoisie allocating hundreds of millions to the army.

But there is yet more. The military budget must be as light a burden as possible for the well-off classes, and as heavy as possible for the poorest classes. This is why the owning classes have introduced those indirect taxes which principally affect humble folk, peasants, artisans, and workers.

Social legislation would undoubtedly be very costly if all just demands were to be satisfied. It is impossible to completely avoid it out of fear of the proletariat. For the owning classes, however, it must not be too extravagant, and for that reason it is necessarily insufficient, and the workers must in addition bear part of its cost.

This is, then, what the big capitalists, mine-owners and owners of the steel mills, metallurgical plants, and textile mills, and shipbuilders and bankers think.

Now anyone will understand that this class's inclination in favor of more steel plate and soldiers, and a more powerful colonialism, and its aversion towards beneficial social reforms, will be more powerfully manifested as the stakes get bigger and as the interests of this class become more preponderant. A powerful imperialism and militarism, then, go along with an insufficient social reform policy.

The class of Junkers acts in a similar fashion. Insofar as it is composed of country gentlemen with mostly provincial outlooks, it is indifferent to colonialism and the drive for a powerful navy; but to the extent that these policies offer it new fields of authority with lucrative administrative posts, it is slowly being reconciled, as a government party, to these policies. The army, on the other hand, in which it occupies all the higher ranks, is its own private domain; if it is sovereign in the army, it is indispensable to the bourgeoisie as a result of the latter's fear of the proletariat. Prussia has led the way as a military State; its position as a great power rest upon the army, and this is why the Junkers are always demanding hundreds of millions more for the army.

It is therefore more easily understood that the money needed for the army has to be drawn from indirect taxes, and from customs duties, since these customs duties also yield millions personally to the Junkers; without customs duties, they would have gone bankrupt long ago.

The Junkers are deadly enemies of the working class and the worst opponents of social reform. They view the peasants who extracted themselves from their despotism by fleeing to the cities as escaped slaves. A faster-paced rural exodus would amount to an improvement in their situation; and it is only this exodus which obliges the Junkers to set limits on their mistreatment of the agricultural workers, who would otherwise all flee.

The middle class has a different attitude towards this question.

It by no means has such a great interest in armies and navies, and even less in colonies. Trade with the colonies is minor and, as commercial outlets for industry, they have little importance.

The middle class, which is composed of small manufacturers, shopkeepers, craftsmen, and peasants, is fully capable of getting State and municipal jobs, or jobs with the big industrial and trading firms, for those members of its families who cannot be employed in the family business, so that its interest in army, navy and colonies, which is of merely secondary importance, will be further limited.

Most members of the middle class, however, follow the politics of the class above them, and we see the parliamentary representatives of the shopkeepers and the peasants, the centrists and the liberals, generally vote for arsenals, armor plate, and colonial budgets.

Does this not contradict what we said above, that is, that the development of the productive forces totally transforms the needs of men, of classes and, for that very reason, their politics, as well? A German peasant or petit bourgeois has no great need for colonies and navies: why does he so enthusiastically pay higher taxes for them?

To successfully address this difficulty, we must take into consideration the fact that a large part of the middle class is totally dependent on capital. Not only because it supplies the employees for private and State services, but especially because it lives on credit. The peasants and shopkeepers most of all. Capital which is available because it is surplus capital means cheap credit for them; flourishing industry and trade produce a surplus of capital. Thus, for this part of the middle class, the following tactic prevails support as much as possible anything the State and capital seem capable of doing: army, navy, colonies.

A large part of the middle class, such as the small manufacturers, artisans who employ manual laborers, peasants who employ servants, and many shopkeepers, live more directly from the exploitation of the workers. With the big capitalists they have in common the exploitation of the workers and experience it first-hand; if their tax burdens are increased for funding social reform, their existence will become more difficult; this is why they fight against the workers.

A large part of the middle class therefore does not have a direct, but an indirect, interest in militarism and imperialism. It does have a direct interest in the exploitation of the workers.

This is how things stand with that part of the middle class which derives more benefits than inconveniences from capitalism. It is otherwise in regard to that part of the middle class which is closer to the proletariat. The poor peasant, the small-scale tenant farmer, the craftsman of modest means, the owner of a small shop, and the low-level employee, without reliable incomes, also depend on capital, but only in the sense that they are oppressed by it. They have no credit; on the contrary, they are neighbors of the proletariat, upon whose business they must often subsist. They are therefore against militarism and imperialism and, although not quite with the same consistency as the workers, in favor of social reforms.

And as technological development causes the ranks of the proletariat to swell, as the danger increases, for the impoverished middle class, of falling into the proletariat, and the pressure of the State and capital becomes stronger, the thought of these layers of the middle class also changes, its will is increasingly turned against capital.

This part of the middle class thus does not have a direct, but an indirect interest in social reforms.

And since the higher layers of the middle class do not have a direct interest in big capital, and the lower layers do not have a direct interest in social reforms, the political thought of all of these layers is uncertain and fluctuating. It is just as likely for the higher layers to lean a little towards the side of the workers as it is for the lower layers to lean a little towards the side of the capitalists, and this, of course, temporarily. And these layers easily become the playthings of social climbers and schemers.

The effect of the relations of production and property are here reflected quite clearly.

The working class—we hardly need to point out—has neither a direct nor an indirect interest in imperialism, militarism, or colonialism. The latter exploit the workers and make social reforms difficult or impossible. War and national rivalry shatter the international solidarity of the workers, the mighty weapon with which, as we shall prove below, they will defeat capitalism.

Imperialism and militarism are the spoiled and pampered children of the big bourgeoisie, and the mortal enemies of the proletariat. The middle class vacillates between love and hate, and for the most part follows behind the powerful.

Radical social reform is the nightmare of the wealthy, and the springboard to power for the workers. The middle class oscillates between these two poles.

This is how the relations of production and property are reflected in the political ideas of the classes. For modern technology grants big capital the monopoly, the major properties; it makes the middle-class dependent on capital or allows it to drift between property and poverty; it deprives the proletarians of all personal property, and all personal power.

The political thought of the classes is the mental reflection of the process of production, with its property relations.

Objection

It seems quite mechanistic to suggest that entire classes of thinking men should be obliged to think the same way. This is what our adversaries put forth as an objection.

But anyone who reflects, even for an instant, upon the fact that the classes are moved by their interest, that their class interest is for them the question of existing or not existing as a class, will be neither surprised nor discomfited by this objection. For classes defend their own existence. If the individual must do everything possible to preserve his existence, this is all the truer of a class which, through its cooperation and social organization, is a thousand times more powerful than an individual.

But each man ultimately conducts the class struggle within the limits of his capabilities. The worker only needs to look around him to note that the lively, passionate mind and the passionate heart are more responsive to the call of highly developed technology than the languid, the fearful or the cowardly. The technological revolution advances rapidly, men follow behind a little more slowly. In the end, however, the masses follow, in the end the whole world follows. The power of the social forces of production is omnipotent.

Today one plainly sees millions of proletarians following modern technology, at first slowly, then faster, and joining social democracy in mass.

The individual therefore has great importance in the evolution of society; the energetic, the passionate, the sensitive, the brilliant, and the diligent, accelerate the progress of a class, while the fools, the slow and the indifferent, retard it; but no man, however brilliant, active or ardent he may be, can divert society in a direction opposed to technological development, and no imbecile, no slacker or apathetic person, can halt the current. Social existence is omnipotent. The individual who resists it is crushed, and his resistance itself will be determined by social existence.

E. *Customs and Morality*

Now that we have finished with the so-called lesser domains of the mind, we shall move on to the so-called higher domains: customs, social morality, religion, philosophy and art. These domains are set above the others by the ruling classes because the latter are all-too connected to matter, while the former seem to soar above all material things. Law, politics and natural science, although mentally elevated, nonetheless deal only with the terrestrial, with material relations and things, things which are often ugly. Religion, on the other hand, along with philosophy, religion, morality and art, seems to be purely mental, beautiful and sublime. A lawyer, a parliamentarian, an engineer or a professor seems less noble than an artist, a priest or a philosopher.

We should not want to give our support to this classification. But it is true that, for us as well, art, philosophy, religion and morality are more difficult domains. Precisely due to the fact that the ruling classes have transformed these domains into supernatural, purely mental spheres, without any link to the earth or society, and because this opinion has insinuated itself into everyone's mind as a prejudice, it is more difficult to demonstrate in this case as well the relation between thought and social existence. We must be twice as lucid in this case, since it affects the interests of the workers twice as much. To grasp the truth on this point makes for tough fighters.

We shall begin with the simplest of the four domains: customs. Here one must clearly distinguish between customs and morality. Customs constitute prescriptions for particular cases, while morality is something general. Among the civilized peoples, for example, it is customary not to go about completely naked, while to love your neighbor like yourself is morality. We shall deal with the simplest morality after having examined customs.

Two clear, very general examples, drawn from our era, and which the worker always has before his eyes, show how customs are transformed by the change of the relations of production.

In the past it was customary for the working class not to bother with public affairs. Not only did the workers have no influence on the government, they did not even think about it. It only drew their attention during times of great tension, during a war against the foreigner or when the kings, the princes, the nobility, the clergy or the bourgeoisie fought among themselves; then, everyone tried to win the workers over to their side; there were thus moments when the workers felt that their interests were also at stake; they would then participate, or allow themselves to be used. But this never led to an enduring political interest among the workers.

All of this is totally different now. Not only do many workers participate in political life but, in the countries where the proletariat has been educated by social democracy, the proletariat has become the class which is most actively involved in politics.

In the past, it was customary for the worker to stay home during the evening; now, the custom is—increasingly so—for the worker to go to a union or party meeting or a gathering of his proletarian cultural association at this time of day.

These customs result from class interest, and class interest is born as a consequence of property relations. In the past it was also in the interest of the ruling classes for the workers to be moderate, peaceful, modest and humble, and for them not to worry about politics except on special occasions. And because the working class was weak due to the technological level of those times, it allowed this status to be imposed upon it by the ruling classes. The priests, government lackeys, schools and, later, the newspapers, preached this attitude to the workers.

The interest of the working class is different now; technology has transformed it, and also made it strong enough to stop listening to the bosses. Thanks to class interest, customs have changed: now, the worker who is not organized is a dull and indifferent worker, a bad worker; but the passionate man who fights for the organization is a good worker.

Therefore—and is this not clear for everyone?—someone is classified as good or bad in accordance with the current custom.

Today the opposite of what was good in other times is good. To be outside, in the street, in a meeting or at a demonstration, is now good. For now technology promises victory to the working class, and the victory of the workers is good for them and good for all of society.

When our comrade Henriette Roland-Holst said that the conceptions of good and bad "are a game of musical chairs", she was never forgiven. But a steady examination of the facts, instead of righteous indignation at the drop of a hat, leads to the observation that different peoples and classes—or the same peoples and classes in different eras—have called the same things good or bad. All of history is replete with such instances. Here we shall only call attention to the customs which regulate the relations between the sexes and marriage, which are different for different peoples and classes or vary from era to era.

Now let us take another very general example drawn from our era. Besides the working class which aspires to advancement, another part of humanity is seeking the freedom of social mobility: women. How did it come about that women, who until not so long ago were educated solely with a view towards domestic labor and marriage, are also striving, hundreds of them, for another goal: a field of activity in society?

In the proletarian woman, this is a result of big industry. Machine labor is often so easy—even if it becomes hard as a result of its duration—that women and children can do it. The father's wages were not enough; the women and children had to go to the factory so that, thanks to their efforts, the family's pay would be sufficient. This is how proletarian women entered the factories and their number has been increasing ever since.

As a consequence, the contents of the minds of women have changed. The socialist idea, the highest point of the labor which they carry out, has also insinuated itself into their heads. In some countries, like Germany, proletarian women have come a long way along the road of socialist organization; they have begun to take this road in every capitalist country. The working class women and the young workers have become comrades in struggle with the men in the political party and the trade union! How unlike other times, when the woman sewed, washed clothes, cleaned the house and took care of the children, and never did anything else!

And it has also gotten into the heads of the socialist women of the working class that there will be a time when women and young people will be completely autonomous socially, and completely free as producers. In the society of the future, no one, neither male nor female, will have a master, either in marriage or in the workplace, anywhere. Individuals will rub elbows as free and equal beings.

And this idea, too, was given to women by the process of production.

The bourgeois woman also aspires to freedom. For her, as well, this idea comes from the process of production. First of all, when big industry took off, women's housework was diminished. Big industry produced all kinds of things so cheaply, such as lighting, heat, clothing, and food, that no one needed any longer to make these things or prepare them at home; secondly, competition has been so fierce that the wives and children of the petit-bourgeoisie have had to go to work and have sought positions in schools, offices, telephone switchboards, pharmacies, etc.; thirdly, among the bourgeoisie the number of marriages has been reduced due to the violent struggle for existence, desires for a better life and the search for pleasure and luxury. All of these things are consequences of the modern mode of production.

This is why the mind of the bourgeois young woman is oriented towards greater social mobility; her thought has been modified. Compared to her grandmother, she is a new human being.

While the proletarian woman, as a result of the place she occupies in the social process of production, has in mind the liberation of the proletariat and, for that very reason, the liberation of all of humanity, the bourgeois feminist only thinks of the liberation of the bourgeois woman. She wants to lead her to power within bourgeois society; she wants to give her capitalist power, which is evidently only possible if she economically and politically oppresses the workers as energetically as the male bourgeoisie currently oppresses them.

The feminist does not want "to free woman from property, but to procure for her the freedom of property", she does not want "to free her from the filth of profit, but to give her the freedom of competition". The working class woman wants to free herself and all the other women and all men from the pressure of property and competition and thus to really free all human beings.

Even if the contents of the minds of these two women are as different as a lamp is compared to the full light of the sun, their thoughts are nonetheless born from the process of production; their thoughts are only distinguished by the different property relations in which the two "sisters" find themselves.

What passionate feelings are inspired in us by the complete liberation of woman, the liberation of the worker, the liberation of humanity! What passion and what resolve they awaken in millions of people, what wellsprings of energy they cause to flow within us! And what magnificent golden and sunset-colored dreams they bring us in the hours of rest that follow after the fight! It might seem that it is the mind of man which has, by its own effort, given birth to all this energy, this mad combativity and these enchanting dreams! But let us never forget, dear friends, that this powerful will of the proletariat, this joy in victory and this stubborn hope after defeat, this extravagant idealism of the workers—the most elevated, the greatest and the most magnificent, yes, the most magnificent by far, because it is the most conscious and therefore the most profoundly idealist expression of the mind that the world has ever known—that these most beautiful mental phenomena are of a piece with labor, with the tools of labor, which, for their part, are rooted firmly in the earth.

These two examples show, on the basis of the two most important changes affecting customs in our time, just how correct our doctrine of historical materialism is. Now we shall address general morality. Before we do so, however, in order to prepare the ground for this next step, and to make the whole issue more comprehensible, we shall first take an example which is not one of the customs of the everyday world of work, like attending workers meetings or female office work, nor is it part of those supposedly higher realms of morality, like loving one's neighbor, love for the truth, etc.

We shall use love of one's country, patriotism, as a bridge between these phenomena.

In this feeling as well, in this thought, we see that a powerful transformation has taken place in our times and, once again, it has principally affected the workers.

In the past, when the working class did not yet represent any kind of autonomous social force whatsoever, it was patriotic, that is, it did not know any better than to follow the ruling classes of its respective countries in wars with foreign powers. It is true that it is not likely that the proletarians of years past and the sons of the peasants and the bourgeoisie of other eras, who enlisted in the army or the navy, did so out of a passionate love for their fatherlands. The majority did so because of coercion and poverty, through lack of a better way to earn a living, but the working classes could hardly have known how to do anything else then, or even what they should have done. The idea never arose in their minds that they could declare themselves to be an autonomous force against war and prevent it, even when the ruling classes wanted war, since they were politically and economically an appendage of the ruling classes. They were not strong enough either numerically or organizationally to form their own idea concerning this question, and even less so when it came to implementing such an idea in practice. Even where they fought to preserve the peace, they habitually did so as defenders of a part of the ruling classes, who saw more advantages to be gained from peace than from war, and carried out their struggle under the slogan that this would be good for the fatherland, that this idea and this activity constitute the real love for the fatherland.

In reality neither war nor such love for the fatherland were very often of any sure use or advantage to the working classes in general. In the past, just like today, it was they who often had to foot the bill with their blood, their lives, and their modest possessions which were torn from them by means of burdensome taxes or which were devastated by war. Even so, in their conceptions they followed the ruling classes and embraced the slogans that were preached to them, such as love for the independence of their country, love of the fatherland or the reigning dynasty, without offering any well-delineated opposition.

How all this has changed! In every country one can daily witness the increase in the number of workers who understand that wars against civilized and uncivilized peoples are only fought for the benefit of the bourgeoisie; that the bourgeoisie only preaches love for the fatherland in order to make the workers docile tools of war; that the end and result of all wars is augmented pillage of the working class or the spread of exploitation to even more workers; that an international war of the peoples is a danger for the workers of the victor nation as well as the vanquished.

"War"—so thinks the modern worker—"is in the interest of the bourgeoisie. Production, that is, the capital invested in production, has become so enormous that it seeks markets and territories as destinations for its money and wants, by means of war, to eliminate some and find a distant use for the rest. But it cannot succeed without collecting ever more burdensome taxes, paying me a lower wage, making me work harder and longer and not providing me with any reforms, or giving me regressive reforms. It is in my interest, on the other hand, to have higher wages, shorter working hours, and progressive legislation and not to have to bear customs duties on foodstuffs or taxes on consumer goods. I must therefore be against war. Furthermore, it is in my interest for my comrade on the other side of the border to enjoy the same benefits, since in that case the industry of his country would not be able to compete unfairly with poverty wages; then, their trade union will become stronger and I will be able to use it as a model to reinforce my trade union and I could even join an international union. And if the workers' political party is powerful there, this will be a stimulus for us to make ours stronger as well, and we will be able to form an international association of all the workers political parties with the same goal and for mutual aid. But if war breaks out, our economic power will be annihilated and the bourgeoisie will sow hatred among us."

The development of industry and world trade has transformed the workers into an autonomous force capable of achieving its goal on its own. But this development, because it has caused capital to metamorphose into a vast power which overwhelmingly dominates every country, has resulted in a situation where the workers can only defeat capital if they act internationally. It is impossible for the workers of one country to defeat their capitalists without the capitalists of the other countries moving heaven and earth to come to the aid of their class comrades. This is now made crystal clear by the international employers' federations. Taking these causes and motives into account, the socialist workers have come to understand that love for the fatherland is no longer their slogan, and that they must take up the watchword of workers international solidarity.

Technology, that is, the currently-attained stage of development of the process of production, makes it necessary for the capitalists of each country either to monopolize the colonial markets, or to obtain the largest possible share of these markets for themselves.

Technology, that is, the currently-attained stage of development of the process of production, makes it necessary for the workers of each country to stand in opposition to this trend because war and colonialism are always accompanied by an increase in the exploitation of the proletariat.

Although all the capitalists are fighting among themselves over markets, technology has reconciled their interests wherever it is essential to oppress the workers.

Technology has organized the workers of every country and has shown them that their interests are the same for all of them wherever it is a matter of expressing the solidarity of all the workers.

Therefore, the owners are for war and oppression of the workers, the workers are for international prosperity and international workers unity.

The working class is therefore certainly not patriotic in the same way as the bourgeoisie, that is, in the sense which has always been attributed to this word under capitalism and which means: love only for your own country; scorn, disdain or hatred for the foreign country.

Modern capitalism is exclusively patriotic out of greed. It does not really consider patriotism to be a virtue, nor does it really think the fatherland is sacred, since it definitely stole the fatherlands of the inhabitants of Transvaal, the Philippines, India, the Dutch East Indies, China, Morocco, etc. It imports Poles, Galicians, Croats and Chinese in order to put pressure on the wages of its compatriots, who are sons of the same fatherland.

It demands of the oppressed class a love for the fatherland which it does not itself feel. The bourgeoisie's love of the fatherland is greed and hypocrisy.

Such a love for the fatherland is undoubtedly totally foreign to the socialist proletariat.

Basically, all love of the fatherland as it is understood by the bourgeoisie is foreign to the worker.

Naturally, the worker wants to preserve his language, which is the only one with which he can find work. But this is not the patriotism which the bourgeoisie demands of him. The worker also loves the natural surroundings, the climate and the air of his country, amidst which he was raised since infancy. But this is not the patriotism which the bourgeoisie requires of him, either. The patriotism which the bourgeoisie wants to impose upon the worker is the patriotism thanks to which the worker docilely allows himself to be used as an instrument of war by the bourgeoisie and allows himself to be massacred by the bourgeoisie when the latter is defending its profits, or is trying to grab the profits of other capitalists or the property of unarmed populations. This is bourgeois patriotism, and it is completely foreign to the socialist workers. In the bourgeois sense of the word, the worker has no fatherland.

Whenever international incidents break out the worker asks himself, what is in the workers' interest, and this, and only this, determines his judgment.

And since at this time the interest of the class of workers demands a general preservation of peace, the policy of the workers presents itself as the means of protecting all nations. If peace endures and the working class comes to power in every country, then there is no longer any possibility that one country will conquer another; next, it would only be a matter of the progressive disappearance of borders and disputes, by organic methods, without violence. Until that point is reached, international social democracy assures the existence of every nation.

And in those rare cases where the proletariat approves of a war—to destroy despotism, in Russia for example—it will not be the patriotism of the bourgeoisie that will be put to work, but the love of the international proletariat.

The working class, which is blazing the trail to socialism, can calmly oppose its goal to the chauvinist patriotism of the bourgeoisie, which pursues filthy lucre, and its hypocritical pacifist farces: the international unity of the workers and therefore of all men, eternal peace for all peoples. The bourgeoisie's goal is limited, just as a country or a little piece of land is limited in relation to the planet; but it is also false and unattainable because the capitalist owners of the countries fighting over the spoils will continue to fight among themselves as long as there are spoils to be had. The goal of social democracy is sublime, pure and resplendent, but it is also really attainable; the working class cannot desire anything but peace among the workers since peace is in their interest and is also the precondition of their victory.

What a change in comparison with the past! The worker of the past thought by slavishly following the lead of the limited ideas of his masters; today's worker embraces the world, all of humanity, he is independent of his masters and fights against them.

And the machine brought about this whole transformation; it is the machine that is responsible, since it engendered and organized millions of proletarians.

Observation

We have already discussed above the fact that the patriotism of the working classes was in past times derived not from their interests, but from the interests of the ruling classes, whose dependants they were. And so it will always be: as long as a class does not have the power to defend its most profound real interests, as long as the interest of another class is in the last instance its own interest, its thought will be largely determined by the thought of the ruling classes. The patriotism of the past was a clear example of this, and still is in many instances. "The ruling ideas of an era", Marx says, "have always been the ideas of the ruling classes". But from the moment when the oppressed class gets the chance, in a revolution for example, to display its most profound interests, it shows its most profound spirit and rejects the ideas which were imposed upon it by its rulers. And as a class becomes stronger by degrees, in such a way that it can defend its own interests, its world of feelings and thoughts are expressed in an increasingly vigorous manner and, finally, openly and brazenly, without false modesty.

Now we shall address the topic of the "higher" domains of morality. The desire for improvement on the part of the worker, the desire for social juridical equality with men on the part of the woman, and patriotism, are only lower feelings in relation to disinterestedness, the love for one's neighbor, devotion, loyalty, honesty, and justice.

These latter virtues pertain to higher morality, they are morality itself.

What are these virtues? Where do they come from? Are they eternal, have they always lived in men's hearts, or are they just as mutable as all the other mental phenomena we have discussed?

These questions have remained insoluble for man for centuries, since the Greek philosopher Socrates and his contemporaries first posed them.

They also present a special difficulty.

For there is a voice in us which immediately tells us, in many cases, what is good and what is bad. Acts of love for one's neighbor and of self-denial are spontaneously produced on their own, on the command of this voice. It spontaneously and imperatively prescribes love of truth, faithfulness, and probity for us. Our conscience warns us when we do not listen to this voice. We are proud of ourselves when we have done good deeds, even when no one is aware of them. Moral law and the precepts of duty live in us, and neither education nor the feeling of pleasure can fully explain them.

This imperative and spontaneous character is a specific trait of ethics and morality. No other mental domain possesses such a character, not the natural sciences, law, politics, religion or philosophy, which everyone has to learn because it could not be otherwise.

Attempts have been made to derive moral law from the individual's own experience, from his education, his habits, desire for happiness, a refined egoism or sympathy for others. But no one has ever managed in this way to explain either the origin of that which is imperious in the voice which calls upon us to love our neighbor, or that which is marvelous in the fact that a man could disregard his own existence to save another's.

Since morality cannot be derived from experience, there is nothing left but the habitual refuge of ignorance: religion. Since morality cannot be explained by the earthly road, its origin must be sought in the supernatural. God gave man the sense of the good, the notion of good; evil comes from the carnal nature of man, from the material world, from sin.

The incomprehensibility of the origin of "good and evil" is one of the causes of religion. The philosophers Plato and Kant constructed a supernatural world upon this fact. And even today, when nature is much better understood, when the nature of society appears much more clearly before man's eyes, even today morality, the desire "for good", the aversion towards "evil", are in the end so marvelous for many men that they can only explain it by a "divinity". How many men no longer need God for an explanation of natural phenomena or history, but declare that God is necessary for "the satisfaction of their ethical needs"? And they are right because they understand neither the origin nor the nature of the great moral precepts, and what is not understood but nevertheless considered to be something very noble, is deified.

The noblest moral precepts have been understood, however, in regard to both their nature and their effect, for half a century. We owe our understanding of them to two investigators: the first studied man in his animal existence, the other studied man in his social existence—Darwin and Marx.

Darwin showed that all organisms carry out a struggle for existence against the natural world around them, and that only those organisms survive which acquire the most suitable specific organs for their defense and for their nourishment, and whose organs attain the best division of labor, and are best adapted to the outside world. A large part of the organic world, comprising the animals, has developed in the struggle for existence and has by means of that struggle developed its freedom of movement and its ability to learn. The ability to learn is composed of observation of the details of the environment, discernment of what is similar and what is different in the environment, and the memory of what previously took place. By means of the struggle for existence, the instincts of self-preservation and reproduction have become increasingly more powerful, as have the division of labor, freedom of movement and thought. This is how the instinct of maternal love evolved. Among the animals that, to prosecute the struggle for existence, must live together in societies of greater or lesser size—such as some carnivores, many herbivores and, among the latter, the ruminants and many primates—the social instincts evolve.

Man, also belongs among these species; man, for his part, has only been able to preserve his existence in nature by social means, by living in groups or hordes, and this is also how the social instincts have evolved in man.

But which social instincts have formed in man and animals due to the struggle for existence and have become stronger thanks to natural selection? "They could be different due to the different living conditions of the various species, but a series of instincts constitutes the precondition for the development of any society." There are instincts without which a society cannot survive and therefore these instincts must be developed in every species which, to assure its continuation, must live socially, like man. What are these instincts?

"Above all, self-abnegation, devotion to the community." If this instinct had not arisen, each person would have lived for himself, and would not have put the community above himself; society would have perished under the blows of the natural forces of the environment or hostile animals. If, for example, in a herd of buffalos, everyone did not devote himself to the collective by resisting when a tiger attacked the herd and taking his place in the circle of his comrades, if every individual fled to save his own life without worrying about the community, then that society would be destroyed. This is why spontaneous self-sacrifice is the first social instinct which must arise in such an animal species.

"Then, bravery in the defense of common interests; loyalty to the community; the individual's subjection to the will of the community and thus obedience or discipline; truthfulness towards society, whose safety would be endangered or whose forces would be squandered when led into error, for example, by false signals. Finally, ambition, receptivity to the praise or condemnation of society. All are social instincts we already find in a developed state in animal societies, often in a highly developed state.

"But these social instincts are nothing but the most eminent virtues, morality itself. All that is lacking at the highest level among them is love of justice, that is, the desire for equality. In fact, there is no place for such an evolution in animal societies, because they only know natural and individual inequalities, but not social inequalities produced by social relations." This love of justice, the desire for social equality, is therefore a property found only in man.(3)

Moral law is a product of the animal world; it already existed in man when he was still a gregarious animal; it is very old, since it has existed in man for as long as he has been a social being, that is, for as long as he has existed.

Men have only been able to overcome nature by mutual aid. Men owe everything to mutual aid, to this moral desire for mutual aid, to this moral law, to this social instinct.

Moral law has been spoken in them since the beginning.

"Hence the mysterious nature of this voice in us which, without external stimulus, is not connected to any visible interest. . . . It is certainly a mysterious desire, but no more mysterious than physical love, maternal love, the instinct of self-preservation, the nature of the organism and so many other things . . . which no one would consider to be products of a supersensory world."

"Moral law is an animal instinct just like the instincts of self-preservation and reproduction, hence its force, its energy, which we obey without thinking, hence our rapid decision in certain cases where it is a matter of knowing whether an action is right or wrong, virtuous or immoral, hence the determination and the energy of our moral judgment, hence the difficulty in providing a basis for it when reason begins to analyze actions and question their motives."

Now we clearly see the nature of duty, we see what conscience is. It is the voice of social instincts calling us. And among these social instincts, at the same time the voices of the instincts of self-preservation and of reproduction also echo, and it often happens then that these two instincts enter into conflict with the voice of the social instinct. When, afterwards, the instincts of reproduction and self-preservation become silent because they are satisfied, then the social instinct often still resounds, but this time as remorse. "There is nothing more mistaken than to see in conscience the voice of the fear of one's peers, their opinion, or their physical force. This voice also acts—as we said above—in relation to actions which no one has experienced, and even in connection with actions which appear quite praiseworthy in their surroundings and can also act as the agent of repulsion in relation to actions which have been undertaken out of fear of one's peers and their public opinion. Public opinion, praise or blame, are certainly very influential factors, but their effect already presupposes a particular social instinct, ambition; they cannot produce social instincts."

One can thus see how easy it is to explain this apparently so marvelous domain of the mind, which embraces the highest precepts of morality, how false it is to resort to the supernatural to do so, and how clear it is that the causes of morality are to be found in our earthly animal and human existence.

This, then, is the nature of morality; this understanding we owe most of all to Darwin. But why are the great virtues so different among the different peoples and eras? How can these social instincts have such different effects in each case?

Darwin did not examine this question. We owe our knowledge of this matter above all to Marx.

It was Marx who discovered the principal causes of the change in the effects of social instincts with reference to the centuries of written history, the era of private property, and the era of commodity production.

Marx made it clear that, due to private property which, in turn, is a product of the development of technology, of the increasing division of labor thanks to which manual labor has been separated from agriculture, classes were born, those of the owners and those of the non-owners, whose members have, from the origins of classes down to the present, waged a struggle among themselves for the products and the means of production. Marx has demonstrated that, from non-stop technological development a non-stop struggle is born. He thereby identified the causes, the most important ones for the modern era, of the changes in the effect of moral precepts.

First, competition arises among the private owners, even if they belong to the same class. And this rivalry has a deadly effect on the highest moral precept, the one that states that one must help one's neighbor, that is, that an individual must sacrifice himself for another. This precept becomes a dead letter in a society which rests upon competition. In such a society, the precept becomes an abstract precept of other-worldly, exclusively heavenly origin, which is delightfully beautiful, but which is not followed, and, strictly speaking, is only for Sunday, when shops and factories are closed and only the church is open. It is not possible to accept the market, a position in the firm, work, engaging in competition, and at the same time to obey the internal voice which has been whispering to us since prehistoric times that we must help our neighbor, since two are stronger than one. It is impossible, and any doctrine that says that it can and must be this way leads to hypocrisy.

In his analysis of the commodity and of capitalist production, Marx discovered that the character of those men who produce their products as commodities in isolation from one another must necessarily be hostile and alienated, as a result of relations not between men, but between things, bolts of cloth, sacks of coffee, tons of minerals, mountains of gold; Marx thus shows us the true relation prevailing among men, the real relation and not the one that exists in the poet's imagination or the priest's homilies.

Secondly, however, technological development and the division of labor created human groups whose members, although often competing with one another, nonetheless have the same interests in opposition to other groups: social classes. Landowners as opposed to industrialists, and employers as opposed to workers, have the same interests. Although they may inflict mutual harm upon one another on the market, all the landowners have the same interest in the struggle for the tariff laws on grain, all the industrialists have the same interest in the struggle for protectionist legislation in favor of industrial products, and all the business owners have the same interest in opposition to progressive social legislation for the workers.

Therefore, the class struggle in reality is fatal to a good part of morality, since the moral precept cannot apply to a class which is trying to destroy or weaken our class, and since that class is capable of experiencing neither support for nor loyalty to our class. Within the domains of the class struggle, there can be no question of any moral precepts whatsoever except within a class; the highest moral precept is just as inapplicable to another class as it is towards the enemy in war. Just as no one ever thinks of sacrificing himself for the enemy during wartime, so it would never occur to anybody to help a member of enemy class. Just as it is true that among certain animal species the moral precept only applies to the members of the same herd, so amongst the primitive lineages of humanity it only applied to the members of the tribe, so too in class society it only applies to class comrades, and this only to the extent allowed by competition.

As a result of technological progress and the accumulation of vast wealth on the one side, and legions of propertyless proletarians on the other side, the class struggle between owners and non-owners, capitalists and workers, is becoming increasingly more acute and violent in our era. These days, then, as time passes, it becomes less and less possible for the classes to mutually observe the highest moral precepts. The other great instincts, however, self-preservation and the reproduction of the species, have far and away taken the lead ahead of the ancient social virtues. The instinct of self-preservation leads the capitalist classes to an ever more obdurate denial of providing the workers with what is necessary. They sense that, in the not-too-distant future, they will have to yield everything, all their possessions, all their power, and, out of fear of giving even one inch in that direction, they are increasingly less disposed to yield anything at all. Nor does the worker feel love for his neighbor in regard to the capitalists, since the instincts of self-preservation and love for his children drive him to attack the capitalists and thereby win a magnificent and happy future.

Technological development, the expansion of social wealth and the ongoing progress in the division of labor have advanced so far, and the owning and non-owning classes have become so distanced from one another, that the class struggle "has been transformed into the essential, the most general and the most long-lasting form of the struggle for existence of the individuals in society."

With increasing competition, our social feelings, our feelings with respect to the members of our society, that is, our morality, is in decline. With the class struggle, our social feelings towards the members of the other classes, that is, our morality with respect to them, is undergoing the same degree of attenuation, but with respect to the members of our own class it has become much stronger.

For the class struggle has already reached such a point that, for the members of the most important classes, the good of their class has become identical with the public good, with the good of all of society. In the name of the public good, one only relies upon one's class comrades and one resolutely prosecutes the struggle against the other classes.

If, therefore, the nature of the highest morality consists of self-denial, bravery, loyalty, discipline, attachment to the truth, a sense of fairness and the aspiration to respect and glorify one's neighbor, the effect of these virtues or instincts is continually transformed due to property, war, competition and class struggle.

In order to make this as clear as possible, we shall now apply what we learned from Darwin and Marx to a particular example, from our own immediate environment.

Let us imagine a business owner, the owner of a factory which he also manages, who is engaged in fierce competition with his class colleagues. Can this man follow the highest precepts of morality, those precepts which, according to the bourgeoisie, are eternal, with respect to his class colleagues, the owners of the competing factories? No, he must attempt to preserve or expand his own market share. He can do this by fair or foul means, but he must do this. Perhaps he is by nature a person with a highly-developed social sense, but he does not pay attention to this sense, because his instinct of self-preservation and his concern for his offspring will overwhelm this social sense. In competition, it is often of vital importance to preserve one's market share, and to get more customers. Stagnation amounts to decline.

As competition becomes more acute, that is, as technology and the world market continue to develop, this manufacturer will have less social feeling, he will more obsessively think about self-preservation, that is, the greatest possible profit. The more acute the competition, the greater the danger of failure.

Can this manufacturer follow the highest precepts of morality with respect to his workers? The question is ridiculous. Even if he is a good man by nature, even if he has an especially strong feeling for those who suffer, he will nonetheless be obliged to give his workers a low enough wage to ensure that his factory will produce a big profit for him. No profit, or a small profit, signifies stagnation. The business must grow, now and then it must be modernized; if not, in a few years it will fall behind the other businesses and, after ten years, it will not be competitive. It is therefore necessary to engage in exploitation, and even the gentlest measures, the most favorable for the workers, must also be such that in the end they do not harm the product, profit. We are considering the case of a capitalist who still feels something for his personnel; most are not like that; for most of them, social feeling was killed long ago by the quest for profit, and those who employ more favorable methods also often do so out of guile, out of a well-considered personal interest, in order to chain the workers all the more firmly to the factory and to make them into slaves who will produce even more.

Let us now suppose that the class of workers begins to struggle against this capitalist and his class, that trade unions are formed and strikes break out, that one or another demand is more or less violently asserted; then all social feeling will slowly disappear in this capitalist and his class with regard to those among their contemporaries who constitute the personnel of their businesses; then class hatred towards the workers will be awakened in them and, wherever there is a struggle with the workers (that is, outside of the ongoing competition), class solidarity with the other capitalists will develop.

And this is also subject to change; this spiritual atmosphere becomes denser as technological development proceeds and as the violence of the class struggle simultaneously increases.

Let us suppose that this manufacturer becomes a member of a syndicate, a trust, or a cartel. This is what he often must do for the purposes of self-preservation. Then he assumes the role of despot over his workers who, because his trust has a monopoly, can only find work in that trust and are as a result totally dependent upon it. This capitalist then proceeds to treat his workers in the manner required by his syndicate. When a restriction of production is necessary, the slave is thrown out of work; if circumstances are more favorable, he is called back to the factory; it is not generosity, or love of one's neighbor, but the world market which decides. As we write this, we are witnessing what may be an unprecedented mass layoff of workers. The American trusts are throwing them onto the streets by the hundreds of thousands. And things are no better for the workers in Europe. In most of these capitalists, a social feeling towards the workers no longer exists.

Now let us take as a second example a politician to whom the capitalist classes have confided the advocacy of their interests in a legislative assembly. Can this person follow the loftiest, allegedly eternal morality with respect to the working class? No, not even if he wanted to do so. For equity, that is, the aspiration to give everyone equal rights, is a moral precept of the highest order. But the capitalist class would perish as such if it were to give equal rights to the workers. Equal rights mean, first of all, equal political rights and, secondly, the common ownership of the land and the means of production. As long as the latter does not prevail, there is no higher law, there is no supreme justice. Could a bourgeois politician achieve such a goal? No, because to do so would be class suicide. He must refuse.

The more passionate the class struggle becomes as a result of technological development, the more numerous, powerful and organized the workers become, the more clearly the possibility of their rule appears, the more determined must the bourgeois politician be to refuse to do anything meaningful on behalf of the workers. The bourgeois politicians must silence their social feeling for the workers and only listen to the voice of self-preservation. Just as it is for the individual capitalist, it is a question of life and death for the whole class.

But as social feeling towards the workers disappears, a feeling of solidarity with the other owning classes is born in the bourgeois politician—we assume he is a representative of one of the owning classes—while struggle and competition prevail with respect to them in other domains.

And this class hatred, as well as this class love, becomes stronger in the politician as the contrast between the owning and non-owning classes becomes more striking, due to technology.

This explains why politicians who, prior to their engagement in practical politics—in an opposition party, for example, or in a young bourgeois party—were full of social feeling for the workers, lose this feeling from the very moment that they have to carry out the practical struggle against the workers. Practice kills this feeling and replaces it with the class solidarity of the owners. Kuyper(4) in Holland, and Millerand, Briand and Clemenceau in France, are outstanding examples of this phenomenon.(5)

Now let us take a worker as our third example.

Can he obey the noble precept of generosity in relation to his employer, to the latter's class and State? No, because he would work himself to death, his wife and children would die of poverty. Poverty, illness and unemployment would ruin him, him and his class. Against this outcome the powerful instincts of self-preservation and the survival of the species both rebel, together with all the most implacable sentiments which are closely related to those instincts, love for his children and his parents. He must not sacrifice himself for the capitalist or the State, since if he allows either untrammeled rule, they will destroy him; they would condemn him to slavery and premature death. History teaches that if the workers do not fight for a better life, the capitalist class will push them to a point where they will be incapable of life or death, and where even the slightest improvements will cost years of efforts. The existence of the workers is often so miserable; unemployment, female and child labor, illness, and competition among the workers are often so unendurable; their lives are so deprived of all spiritual and physical pleasures whose satisfaction would nonetheless be so easy, that surrender to the capitalist class and its State means nothing but the downfall of the worker from that narrow ledge he occupies, a fall to his death. This is why the worker behaves in a manner contrary to the highest moral law with respect to the capitalist class (the law which Christians express as follows: love your neighbor as yourself): he commits himself to the struggle against the ruling class.

And the greater the resistance of the capitalists due to technological development, the stronger their organization in employers' associations, trusts and political parties, the weaker the social instinct towards the capitalist class becomes in the hearts of the workers; just as, in the capitalist class, this instinct is transformed into class hatred.

Let us proceed to imagine that this worker has come to understand class and production relations so profoundly that he becomes a socialist; his higher moral instincts will then become increasingly passionate with regard to the class of non-owners and will grow to the same degree that they will diminish with respect to the capitalists and their society. If he is a man who is gifted by nature with elevated moral sentiments, the latter will be strengthened by the understanding that he and his children, and all his comrades, will only attain happiness if all of them, and he as well, will mutually listen to the voice which calls to loyalty, love of truth, bravery, self-sacrifice, and justice.

And as the misfortune of the class deepens, that is, because of technological development, the greater is the workers' need for a socialist society and the more widespread the owners' resistance to such an outcome, the more the workers' solidarity will grow, the more forcefully will morality speak in the proletariat, the more the proletariat will pay heed to that voice. And therefore, the effect of morality will undergo continuous changes in this instance as well.

Finally, let us suppose the case of a worker who has so expanded the scope of his intellectual development that he feels quite distinctly the happiness which the communist society will bring to all men, the misery which it shall cause to disappear; he will then discover, through his hatred of the owners and his solidarity with the non-owners, a path for his highly elevated moral sentiment. He feels that only when the workers are victorious and realize communist society will moral law be capable of being applied by us towards all men. This is why, in his aspiration and that of his class, to abolish private property, competition and the class struggle, he feels in the bottom of his heart something, even if it is only the first glimmer of dawn of the moral law that will apply to all men. If socialist society is a blessing for the whole world, then the aspiration to hasten its arrival will also already contain something of the universal love for humanity that extends to every nation.(6)

With these examples, which are known by every worker from his immediate experience in real life, it becomes absolutely clear that the effect, the content and the mode of existence of our allegedly supreme and eternal morality is modified in our heads and our hearts in response to the changes which take place in the class struggle, in class relations, that is, in the relations of production and therefore, ultimately, in production and technology. The highest morality is therefore not immutable; it is alive, that is, it changes.

Objection

We have already mentioned the fervor with which the adversaries of social democracy seized upon the contention of Henriette Roland-Holst that the conceptions of good and evil "are a game of musical chairs". What our comrade meant by this expression is that, just as children change places in the game of "musical chairs", so also do the conceptions of good and evil not always apply to the same acts, and that today one finds "good" in the chair where "evil" used to be.

We have now demonstrated with the most comprehensive examples that this judgment is correct. The new female virtues, the new workers' virtues, patriotism, international feeling, are changing what was good has become evil, and vice-versa.

Our adversaries cry out at us: there is an eternal and unchanging morality; its supreme precepts are always the same.

We respond: prove it. Not with exclamations and rhetoric, not with authoritarian arrogance or with spectacular judgments of condemnation, but historically, with facts that the whole world can see and examine.

They cannot.

We, however, have demonstrated, with the support of Darwin and Kautsky, that, first of all, there exists in man a tendency to help his fellow man, a moral precept of purely earthly, and even animal origin, but that, on the other hand, the expression of this moral law is always different due to the struggle over property, competition and the class struggle, and that moral law when applied to class comrades has a completely different content than when applied to class enemies.

The whole world knows this is true; anyone can observe this every day with respect to themselves and others. We have, then, opposed vain assertions with realities.

It clearly emerges from our proofs that, against the enemy, whether the enemy of the tribe, the nation or the class, the highest precepts of morality do not apply; that, to the contrary, the morality which orders us to help our comrades, simultaneously obliges us to destroy the enemy who torments them; and therefore that the precepts of self-sacrifice, solidarity, honesty and loyalty are not applicable to the class enemy.

Our adversaries are also shocked that we should actually say this, and this is why they insult us. But we can again tranquilly draw attention to the fact that they themselves, the conservatives, the liberals, the supporters of the religious parties and the democrats, constantly act in precisely the same way. For day after day, year after year, they deny the absolute necessities of life to the enemies of their class, the workers; they sacrifice nothing of what their class possesses, beyond what is snatched from their grasp by fear of the workers' power; they do not show the least solidarity with the workers but throw them in chains when they try to mobilize and take disciplinary measures against them as in the case of the Dutch rail strike; they are neither honest with nor loyal to them, but in the elections they regularly make promises to them which they do not fulfill. And in the meantime, they are preaching love for one's neighbor, for all neighbors!

We, on the other hand, know from history that whenever someone wanted to help his class or his people, the highest precepts of morality have never applied to the enemy, and we frankly confess that we shall be neither altruistic nor loyal, nor honest in our dealings with the enemy class when the salvation of our class requires it.(7)

Against these observations, it might be objected that, even so, all human feeling is not totally squelched in the class struggle; if, in war, despite the desire to destroy the enemy, the precepts of morality have a certain validity, prisoners are not killed, agreements are abided by and promises are kept, this is all the more true for the class struggle where the adversaries are much closer to one another!

This observation is perfectly just but does not constitute an objection to our observations. For we make it perfectly clear that the precepts of morality as applied to the enemy are only jettisoned when the true salvation of the class demands it. Human feeling is not universally suppressed in the class struggle, but only when a class judges that such a course is unavoidable for the purpose of preserving its existence. If it is not necessary, the workers are not killed by the capitalist power; if it is necessary, they are killed. In the Prussian mines, they do not employ labor inspectors, because it is feared that then the great masses of miners would become politically and economically too powerful. In 1903, they simply allowed the Dutch rail workers to starve to death, but in 1871 the fighters of the Commune were subjected to mass killings because the bourgeoisie judged that it was necessary for its power to sow a great deal of fear among the proletariat.

The worker, on the other hand, will not lie to or deceive his employer if possible. Generally, it is not in his class interests to deceive him. But where his class interest requires the violation of moral precepts, he will violate them.

But it is precisely regarding this point that objections will be put forth by the social democrats themselves, by workers in the midst of struggle. They acknowledge that the capitalists are constantly violating moral precepts in the class struggle, that they act in bad faith, falsely, insincerely, and brutally against the oppressed class in order to preserve its oppression. But socialism signifies precisely a higher morality; the fighting workers do not need such means, and when they do on occasion employ them, we must hold them accountable for it.

In this objection there is only one correct point, and that is that the working class is much less obliged than the ruling class to violate moral precepts; this is based on its situation as a weak and oppressed class which rises thanks to economic development, while the ruling classes try in vain to stay in power. But in its generality, this observation is nothing but one more proof that one can always easily detect the violation of morality by one's class enemy, but it is very hard to discern such violations by one's own class. Some examples will show us—if we want to clearly face up to the truth—that we do not condemn violations of moral precepts when they are undertaken essentially in the interest of our class, but, on the contrary, we celebrate them as noble deeds.

Let us imagine a factory that pays low wages, and a trade union that wants to struggle for higher wages. Let us suppose that this can only be achieved by means of an unannounced strike. A few days before the strike is scheduled to begin, when everything is ready, the owner of the factory notices something; he approaches a worker and asks him if something is afoot. If the worker responds evasively, the manufacturer will immediately understand what is going on and will call for strikebreakers. For this reason the worker lies; he denies that anything is going on and says he knows nothing. In the eyes of the manufacturer, he is evil, but in the eyes of the workers he is good. Such cases are common. It can be a good thing to lie.

Let us imagine an office employee in a government ministry and let us assume he is a social democrat. A proposal that constitutes a threat to his class comes into his hands. He steals it and conveys it to the Vorwärts editorial office. We consider this to be a praiseworthy act. Dishonesty with respect to the enemy class can therefore be a virtue in the eyes of your own class.

In 1903, many of Holland's rail workers came to an agreement to stop rail traffic after a particular signal was given. This was an act of disloyalty to the railroad companies. For us, however, it was an act of the most elevated kind of loyalty.

After the Dutch rail strike, a parliamentary commission was appointed to investigate the situation of the railroads and it discovered the horrible conditions prevailing in that industry. But its report was kept secret, and the government did not feel obliged to intervene using legal methods. Some office employee or functionary, or perhaps a printer who acquired a copy of this report, gave a copy of it to the secretary of the rail workers union, and the union secretary publicized the contents of the report in speeches and numerous meetings. At that time no worker, no social democrat, disapproved of this act; everyone felt that loyalty to one's own class was more important than loyalty to the capitalists.

How many more examples do we need to contrast our truth with hypocritical bourgeois morality! One more: the workers of the Commune did not hesitate to fight the reactionary classes with their weapons. This was a crime in the eyes of the enemy, the greatest courage and self-sacrifice in our eyes. Much the same can be said for our comrades, the combatants of the Russian revolution.

On the other hand, one could proffer numerous examples of how our adversaries infringe upon moral precepts in the class struggle. We repeat: all classes conduct themselves in the class struggle in accordance with a custom which stands in contradiction with the universal morality preached by the bourgeoisie. The capitalist classes are constantly lying to, cheating, and robbing the working class; they do these things in their capacity as ruling elements, and it is for this reason even more serious; they must do this, because their social system is based upon such conduct. But the working class is also often obliged to be disloyal, insincere, etc., in the class struggle.(8)

Here it is necessary to insert one more observation to make ourselves perfectly clear. We have shown that all classes use bad faith as a means in the class struggle and that they consider this to be moral. But the owning class is obliged by its situation to employ the lie much more often than the working class as a method of struggle. This is true not only regarding the everyday struggle, but also and above all in connection with scientific truth concerning society itself.

The capitalist class is in decline, the working class is on the rise; this is how the process of production wants it to be. But the acknowledgment of this fact would be, for the bourgeoisie, one part of the decline which it denies is taking place. This is why it hates all the truths which refer to this aspect of its decline and tries to combat them wherever it still holds sway. But since the process of production moves inexorably forward, this is not possible except by means of lies. Out of class interest, it instinctively seeks out the lie and in the best cases it believes it to be the truth. The working class, on the other hand, has an interest in the truth in all domains of society. It advances thanks to social forces; it therefore wants to understand them; this knowledge is beneficial for it because it becomes a new force for its advancement.

Everything that affects the domain of the class struggle is for us an object of honest study in search of the truth. We do not fear clear understanding because our victory is becoming more certain.

Therefore, we do not always speak the truth; in the struggle, we must sometimes be—our examples have proven this—insincere with respect to the adversary; but we always seek the scientific truth concerning society, we never conceal it. We also do this out of class interest.

This is a major difference between the proletariat and the bourgeoisie.

Here, too, the worker must decide for himself which side he wants to be on, that of the capitalists or that of the socialists.

There is, however, yet one more thing that requires clarification, and this will allow us to put this difficult point behind us.

The attentive reader might ask: if the same highly ideal morality does not float before the eyes of all men, and if morality is not eternal and does not always take the same form, then is the ideal of equality, universal love of one's neighbor, happiness and justice really the same for the whole world?

Marxism responds as follows: it is so only in appearance; one always finds the same words in human history: liberty, equality, justice, fraternity. It seems, then, that the ideal is always the same.

But upon closer examination, it is clear that the cause of this appearance resides in the fact that, since the advent of class society, all ruling classes have always preserved enslavement, inequality and injustice, and all the dominated and oppressed classes, from the moment that they became aware of this and began to flex their muscles, have demanded justice, liberty and equality. Since there has always been oppression, there has always been a sense of liberty and equality. But if we look behind the slogans, behind the words, we find that the liberty and the equality proclaimed by some people was completely unlike the liberty and the equality proclaimed by others, and that the difference derived from the class and production relations within which the various oppressed peoples lived. We have already proven this above thanks to the examples of Christianity, the French Revolution and social democracy, and therefore need not undertake to provide further proofs.

The moral ideal is also different for different eras and classes. It lives and evolves like all ideas. All morality is, then, like politics, law and other mental products, a natural phenomenon which we understand quite well and which we can trace in its evolution.

Observation

Morality is not a spiritual domain separate from all others. Man is not partly a political being, partly a juridical being, and then, categorized separately, a moral being and, in yet another part, a religious being. Man is a whole which we split into different parts solely for the purpose of understanding him better, to more clearly understand each part considered separately. In reality, political, moral, juridical and religious conceptions are intimately interwoven and all of them together comprise a single spiritual content. For us, then, it is not surprising that they mutually influence one another. Once a political conviction takes shape, it has its own power and it influences juridical conceptions and moral sentiments; once moral sentiments are formed, they have a retroactive effect on political as well as other convictions.

We shall prove this with an example.

As everyone knows, the misery caused by the capitalist system leads many people to abuse alcohol. But capitalism compels the destitute to organize and struggle and thereby creates in them the following kinds of morality: sentiments of solidarity, a greater power of moral resistance, bravery, pride, etc. This morality, these social instincts, lead to abstinence or temperance, and the latter qualities have the effect of making political convictions clearer and the political force of the destitute much greater. Morality has therefore exercised influence on knowledge, thought, ideas concerning legal rights, property, and class struggle.

It is, however, no less correct to maintain that changes in morality derive from the development of the forces of production—for without the latter, the former would never have led to organization and consciousness of its own power—but there is a reactive force among all these spiritual domains which, as a result of their all being rooted in social labor, all influence one another mutually.

Our adversaries often attempt to refute our positions by saying that they call attention to the influence of spiritual causes, religion, morality and science. Social democracy must not allow itself to fall into error because of this objection. It will grant a high degree of recognition to the influence of intellectual forces—otherwise, why would it stir up people's minds so much if it did not believe such activity to be of any use?—but it will also examine how this intellectual force has been put into motion prior to its exercising this influence. And then it will discover that the development of production and of the relations of production is the ultimate cause of its being put into motion.

F. *Religion and Philosophy*

Every religion—there were and there are thousands of kinds of religions—every religious sect, considers itself to be the true religion. Nothing, however, is more dependent upon the evolution of technology, nothing is changed more by the latter than religion. We shall demonstrate this by means of a brief account.

When technology did not yet dominate the forces of nature and, to the contrary, nature almost totally dominated man, when the latter still used only what he found in nature as tools and was only capable at first of manufacturing a few such tools, he worshipped the forces of nature, the sun, the sky, lightning, fire, mountains, trees, rivers and animals, as a function of the importance conceded to these factors by the tribe. The same is still true among the so-called primitive peoples: the inhabitants of New Guinea, which the Dutch are currently colonizing on behalf of the capitalists, worship the starchy pith of the sago palm tree as their god; they believe they are the descendants of this material.

But after the development of technology, after the invention of agriculture, after the warriors and priests seized power and property, after the appearance of rulers and ruled and therefore of classes, after man was no longer completely subject to nature, but to man, and above all to men of higher status, since man has exercised power, the true nature gods disappeared and were transformed into imaginary creatures in the form of powerful men. The divine forms found in the works of the ancient Greek poet Homer are powerful princes and princesses, the prince being deified bravery, the princess being deified prudence, beauty or love. The nature gods became magnificent men. Technology gave power to men; the gods became powerful men.

But when the Greeks, as a result of their technology, which continually improved, had covered their country with trade routes, the sea with fleets and, especially, the coasts with cities, when trade and industry prospered, when, in short, commodity society was born, in which everything, land, products, tools, ships and carts, became commodities destined for trade, then neither sun, or fire, or mountain or tree was marvelous or the most important of all, all-powerful or mysteriously divine for this society anymore; nature was now too much within its power for such views. During that era, it was no longer human strength or skill, bravery, or beauty, as in Homeric times; these physical characteristics no longer possessed their former importance in a society which rested on competition. Something else, however, appeared in this society as more important than anything else, dominating everything, the most marvelous of all, and so it was for Greek society. This was the mind, the human mind.

In commodity society, the mind is the most important factor. It counts, it invents, it measures and weighs, sells, makes a profit, subjects, dominates men and things. In commodity society, the mind is at the center of life, like the starchy pith of the sago palm tree among the Papuans and like beauty and strength in Homer. It is what expresses power.

The first great philosophers of Greek commodity society, Socrates, and Plato, often said that what interested them was not nature, but only the phenomena of thought and the soul.

This step is a clear consequence of the technological development which created commodity society.

There were strange phenomena in the human mind which were not understood. What were the universal ideas found in the mind, where did they come from? What was the magnificent force in thought which operated with such ease and so prodigiously with these universal ideas? Where did it come from?

It could not have come from the earth, because only particular things are found on the earth, and not universal ones. And what were the moral sentiments, those conceptions of good and evil which are found in the human mind, but which are so difficult to apply in commodity society? For what is good for one person is bad for another: the death of one is bread for the other, and the advantage of one private person often means harm for the community.

All of these things constituted enigmas which, for the great thinkers like Plato, Socrates, Aristotle, Zeno and so many others, were insoluble in other times, which could not be explained by nature and experience, and which had to lead to the assertion that the mind was of divine origin.

The social instincts and sentiments are so important for men that, when they are shattered by commodity society, men need to undertake an investigation to find out where they come from and how they can be recreated. They are also so vigorous, so splendid and so sublime, that acting in accordance with them provides such pleasure and such an increase in strength that when it becomes possible to do so, their magnificence receives an ideal splendor and it seems that they must necessarily come from another, superior world.

To explain to them, a heaven full of gods, such as was the case with the numerous natural phenomena, was no longer necessary; one god was enough. And since "good and evil" are mental concepts, this god is easy to represent as mind.

In commodity society, intellectual labor dominates manual labor. Management, the administration of the business and the State, are the affair of the intellectual laborer; the artisan, when he is not a slave, is of lower rank. This also led people to see the divine in the mind, and to consider god as a mind.

To this was added the fact that, in the commodity-producing society, every man becomes an individual who is in competition with the others. Every man thus becomes the most important object for himself and—since he feels, reflects and ascertains everything in his mind—his mind becomes the most important part of this object. This was most conducive to making the men of this society perfectly fitted to consider the mind as divine and god as an individual mind which exists by itself.

Technology had led man so far that he no longer deified a bull, a cat, or an ibis, a tree, or a human physical attribute, but not so far that he was capable of understanding the nature of thought and the conceptions of "good" and "evil". This is why, in the past, this mental and moral complex which was all-powerful yet incomprehensible in that society was declared to be divine. And this has remained unchanged in commodity society up to the present day. "God is a spirit", is still said today, and most moral conceptions even today have a supernatural origin.

As long as the known world of the ancients was not yet a single economic and political whole, that is, one big commodity society, there was naturally room within it for various gods, and also for the gods of nature. But when the world trade of the Greeks, first of all, and later Alexander of Macedon and finally the Romans, had created a world empire which produced commodities throughout the entire Mediterranean basin, one spiritual god was enough, one divine spirit, to explain the whole known world and all the hardships within it, and to cause the nature gods to disappear from it. The Roman technology which penetrated everywhere, Roman trade and circulation, the Roman commodity society, universally repelled the nature gods. And so, too, was the system with only one god, monotheism, discovered in the two philosophical conceptions which had previously been imposed on the great world empire, in the doctrine of Plato and in Stoicism.

And when one particular kind of monotheism penetrated into this zone, one that was specifically suited to the gigantic scale of the general economic collapse, and to the social relations of the Roman Empire in the era of the Caesars, Christian monotheism, it everywhere discovered a fertile field and only had to integrate Greek monotheism as one element within it.

The whole society of the Mediterranean basin had become one commodity-producing society that everywhere presented the same mysteries and contradictions, and everywhere exhibited identical individuals who produced commodities. Everywhere the spirit was what was powerful, marvelous, and mysterious. Everywhere, the spirit was God.

And as primitive foreign peoples, such as the Welsh and the Germans, were integrated into the commodity society, they, too, gradually lost their original religions and also became ripe for Christianity, which attributed all power to one God.(9)

But the Christian religion did not remain the same as it was during its first few centuries. From a religion for one class only, it became the religion of all classes, when production regressed to the state of natural economy and thus when the great community of production for which one god, and one spirit was sufficient to explain the universe had decomposed into a mass of small separate units of production. As medieval society developed, the content of religion was also transformed. Medieval society was the society of landed property, in which men became progressively bound to one another by ties of dependence and in which those who were dependent did not sell the surplus product of their manual labor but gave it to their lords. The serfs and those who were subject to personal service delivered the products of nature to their noble and religious lords. At the head of secular society was the Emperor, under him the princes, under them the feudal lords, under them the petty nobility, and under the nobles the great mass of serfs and persons subject to personal services. In the Church, which also owned vast landed estates, similar relations prevailed. The Church had evolved from the ancient, impoverished community which consumed in a communist manner, to an enormous institution of exploitation. At its head was the Pope, and under him the most diverse kinds of great religious lords, who were in various grades of dependence upon one another, cardinals, archbishops, bishops, abbots and abbesses, and then the lower grades of the ecclesiastical hierarchy, the monks and the nuns of all kinds, and finally the vast mass of the people, the community. Together, the religious and secular powers formed one great hierarchical society which rested primarily on the supply of the products of nature by the oppressed. And the Christian religion had been transformed into the image of this society, with this mode of production. It was no longer one god which inhabited heaven, but a whole population of spiritual powers. God thundered above all, existing only as one with his son and the Holy Spirit, penetrating and enveloping everything. Under him, in various grades, there were many kinds of angels with diverse functions, and also fallen angels or demons, which had to be busy with evil. Then there were the saints who, as society rested for the most part on the delivery of products of nature and not on commodities, and since society depended on nature (on the weather, for example), were also turned into a new class of subordinate nature gods, all of whom also had their own functions: one saint for vintners, one for the hay, one saint who came to the aid of women in childbirth, etc. God was, consequently, with all these people around him, an image of the emperor or the Pope with the secular or religious powers they wielded. And under all these angels and saints were men, alive and dead: an image of the earthly communities and the earthly population. The relations of production and landed property, the personal dependence of the princes, the nobles, the bishops, the abbots, the serfs and the people, were represented by the ruling classes simply as the result, the creation of precisely a heavenly society which, to speak truly, was incomprehensible but which, precisely as a result of its divine essence, did not need to be understood. And the naïve believers accepted this representation in their desire to understand society, the mysterious humanity as well as "good" and "evil".

Never, in any era we know of, has religion so clearly reflected society. The spirit created a heavenly image of earthly society.

This changed when cities began to get bigger.

The burghers of the cities of Italy, southern Germany, the Hanseatic League, France, Flanders, and the Netherlands became powerful and independent thanks to trade and industry. They freed themselves from the oppressive bonds which had been imposed upon them by the nobility.

The possession of capital, which belonged to them alone, with which they could do as they pleased, transformed them into free and autonomous individuals, no longer dependent upon the favor of a lord. This placed them in a different kind of relation to society than was the case with the serf class, from which many of them had issued, and it was also unlike that of the nobles or the clergy.

As they were conscious of their different relation to society, they also felt a different sort of relation to the world. This called for a new religion, because it was through religion that men expressed their sense of their relation to the world.

Just as they could do as they wished in the world with their capital, which they had acquired with their industry, their technology and their trade, and since they did not acknowledge any economic power above them—and they became more free politically—and since, as individuals, as capitalists, as traders, they could freely hold their heads high in the world, just as they did not accept any intermediaries between themselves and the world, so also did they not want to accept any intermediaries between themselves and God. They protested against such a state of servitude.

They did away with the Pope and the saints and became their own priests. Every man was his own priest; every man was in direct contact with God. This is what Luther and Calvin taught.

It was the protestant religion, that is, bourgeois consciousness, which made its appearance with the development of modern capitalist commodity production and which saw its most powerful growth take place in those countries which followed the bourgeois path of development, France, Switzerland, Germany, Holland, England and Scotland.(10)

In this case as well, religion is again a reflection of social life. Just as the bourgeois is individualist, so also is his religion individualist; his God is as solitary as he is.

The stronger capitalism became, especially after the discovery of America and the East Indies, the more rapid and vigorous was the growth of trade and industry, as less of the home countries' production was devoted to their own needs and more to the foreign market, the more generalized and difficult became the social struggle of each against all under capitalism as a result of constant improvements in the means of communication and instruments of production, and the more solitary man became in economic life and in his spirit as well. With the development of modern capitalism, men increasingly fell under the domination of their products; their products somehow acquire a human power over men; men are dominated as if they were things, and everything has an abstract exchange value in addition to the use value products have for men. In such a society, men have, as Marx says, come to see each other as abstractions; their god had to be transformed into an abstract idea.

Furthermore, with the growth of capitalism, poverty gets worse, society becomes more complicated and harder to make sense of, and it becomes increasingly more difficult to distinguish what is really good from what is really bad for everyone. Introspection, speculation, and spiritualization become the only means by which one can find certainty, stability, and happiness, in the midst of the struggle and activity unleashed by the production of commodities and trade.

As a result, we see that the image of God is becoming more and more isolated, more spiritualized and more abstract. Among the philosophers of the seventeenth century, in Descartes, Spinoza and Leibniz, God became one vast being within which everything exists, and outside of which there is nothing. In Spinoza, who may have set out the most complete philosophical system—it has been likened to a pure, perfectly-cut diamond—in Spinoza, then, God is a vast body with a vast mind, outside of which nothing exists, and which constantly moves and thinks for itself. A reflection of the individualist, bourgeois man.

Knowledge of nature increased along with the development of technology and capitalism; by the seventeenth century nature had been so extensively understood in its true coherence that its incomprehensibility and divinity had been dispelled. The mind, however, the faculty of understanding itself, general ideas and, above all, the ideas of good and evil and the so-called mental sciences, were not yet understood. For this reason, nature and matter slipped more and more into a secondary level in religion. God had become more of a ghostly and abstract spirit, distant from reality. The old Christian contempt for the "flesh" made no small contribution to this development. And the separation between mental and manual labor, which had become more marked as technology advanced and with the spread of the division of labor, within which intellectual labor was reserved for the owning classes and manual labor was reserved for the proletariat, this separation, then, was also the cause, as in the Greek world, of the fact that matter was completely omitted from religion. For all these reasons the philosopher Kant simply designated everything relating to time and space as phenomena without real existence. The philosopher Fichte only recognized one spiritual subject or the ego, the philosopher Hegel posited an absolute spirit which established the world as the manifestation of itself, a world which finally arrives at self-consciousness and reverts to absolute spiritual existence.

Capitalist society isolated the bourgeois individual, it spiritualized him and made him incomprehensible to himself to such an extreme degree that the philosophers of the eighteenth and nineteenth centuries created such a solitary, abstract and incomprehensible god!(11)

Meanwhile, thanks to the invention of the steam engine, the productive forces, the means of communication and, therefore, capital, have undergone tremendous growth. The new technology, in turn, permitted a more effective investigation of nature, which it required. Yet more of nature was revealed to the eye of man, new discoveries were made regarding the coherence of the laws which rule all natural phenomena, the existence of a supernatural being in nature was increasingly rejected and, finally, such a being was completely eliminated from nature.

And then, for the first time ever, the understanding of society also became more profound. Prehistoric times became the object of research, the era of written history was more fully understood, statistics made its appearance, and, for the first time, laws were discerned in human actions. And as what was natural in man became better understood, the supernatural disappeared from him and from society itself just as it had been eliminated from nature.

Technology, the means of communication, the mode of production, and the capital which had accumulated so prodigiously, provided the incentive and the means for the investigation of nature. The vast social questions born from the process of production stimulated man's mind to investigate society. Technology permitted the exploration of deep layers of the earth and distant journeys to the lands of the most primitive peoples, as well as the collection of materials for history and statistics. The mode of production which created needs also created the means to satisfy them.

The class which had the imperious necessity of new sciences to augment its technology and its profits and to defeat the old reactionary classes of the landowners, nobility and clergy, that is, the capitalists of industry and commerce who called themselves liberals in the political arena, this class acquired more and more understanding of the rule of law in the phenomena of nature and society; within this class, religion had almost completely disappeared. What remained within this class which pertained to religion was the idea—which subsisted in the deepest recesses of its conscience, and which had no practical significance—that "maybe there is a god, after all".

Moderns and freethinkers, who are the counterparts in the domain of religion of the liberals in politics, no longer need god to explain notions of "good" and "evil", or, as they say, to satisfy their "moral" needs, and to give birth to the spirit, whose nature is still to this day an enigma to them, of a supernatural nature. For nature and for a good part of human and social life, they no longer need God; science, which rests upon technology, has illuminated these topics sufficiently for them.

In this manner, modern capitalism, because it has so much improved the understanding of the world, has increasingly refined religion since the era of Luther and Calvin, and has made it more nebulous, cut-off from the world, and unreal. I aroused a great deal of opposition in reactionary, liberal and even socialist circles when I wrote that religion had fled with its head bowed from the earth like a fearful ghost. But all I did was to state what was really the case: religious representations are becoming increasingly ghostly. Only the classes in decline, such as the petit-bourgeoisie and the peasants, and the reactionary classes like the big landowners with their ideologues, are still convinced of its representations from centuries past; for most of the members of the owning classes and their intelligentsia only a tiny bit of religion remains, or they pretend to hold fast to it in order to keep the proletariat down, or for some other reason. The knowledge engendered by the development of capitalist production has drained all substance from religion and has only left it with a ghostly, ethical existence.

But that same economic development, which has largely deprived the liberal bourgeoisie of religion, totally deprived the proletariat of religion.

We are only drawing attention to the facts when we assert that the proletariat is becoming increasingly irreligious.

This is socially just as natural as all the other changes in religious thought that we discussed above.

In general, we discovered the reason for religion in the domination of powers which are not understood. The forces of nature, and the social powers which are not understood, but which are nonetheless felt to be dominating forces, are deified.

And now what is happening in relation to this point with the modern proletariat, that is, the industrial worker of the city who lives in the surroundings of capitalist big business?

The factory has allowed him to see with his own eyes that the forces of nature do not represent incomprehensible forces. Man understands and controls them there, he plays with those forces which, untamed, are the most dangerous. Even if the worker does not understand them theoretically, they are under the control of this hand, and he knows that they are understood.

The modern proletarian, furthermore, understands perfectly well those social forces which are the causes of his poverty. The capitalist mode of production unleashed the class struggle in which he participates, and the class struggle has taught him to recognize capitalist exploitation and private property as the causes of his miserable situation, and socialism as his salvation. For him, then, there is nothing supernatural about either nature or society. He feels that there is nothing in either nature or society which he is not capable of understanding, even if society has temporarily deprived him of the possibility of doing so. He also feels that what is currently an overwhelming cause of poverty for him and his class will not always be. But when the sense of an incomprehensible higher power is lacking, religion doe not arise in him, or if he had it before, it dies and disappears. For this reason the socialist worker is not anti-religious, but has no religion, he is an atheist.

If this is already true for the "ordinary" worker, who has neither the time, nor the desire, or the opportunity to devote himself to study, how much more true is it of the worker who is compelled to educate himself due to the class struggle! Precisely because he is a worker, because the poverty of the proletariat compels him to study, he can attain a better understanding of society than a bourgeois professor of political economy, for example. The bourgeois cannot see the truth; he cannot admit that his class is in decline; he cannot even acknowledge the class struggle in which his class will necessarily be on the losing side. The mind of the worker, on the other hand, which can expect everything from the future, is as prepared for the truth as a hunting dog is prepared to hunt.

The worker has impressive resources at his disposal. More than sixty years ago, Marx explained to the proletariat that capital comes from unpaid labor.(12) More than sixty years ago, Marx and Engels unveiled to the proletariat the nature of the class struggle.(13) And then Marx set out in Capital the nature of the whole capitalist production process, which the worker can find explained more clearly and concisely in Kautsky's The Economic Doctrines of Marx and in the Erfurt Program. The bourgeoisie has no such resources of social knowledge. The worker who has quenched his thirst from these springs will no longer see anything supernatural in society. It is not simply something negative that shall take root in him, a lack of religion, but also something positive, a clear and coherent conception of the world.

And if he continues to read and to reflect, he will discover the proof in the works of Marx, Engels, Kautsky, Mehring and many other eminent theoreticians of the fact that the mental life of man is determined by his social existence, that the law is class law, politics is class politics, that good and evil are mutable social notions, in short, the truth of everything we have been discussing in this pamphlet and of everything taught by historical materialism. Then he will also understand the transformations which take place in thought and he will therefore understand his own thought. The man who practically engages in the production of society, with his hands, also penetrates it more thoroughly with his mind.

He understands class thought, and once again it is metaphysical thought which collapses, a bastion of religion, which he learned at home and at the church.

And the proletarian for whom the superficial test given him in the factory, and by the political and trade union struggle, is not enough, can go even further in his understanding!

Joseph Dietzgen, the philosopher of the proletariat, as he has been quite justly called, and a student in his time of Marx, has he not taught the proletariat, on the basis of socialist science, what is mind? Has he not explained to the workers the enigma by which the bourgeoisie is still dumbfounded, that is, the nature of human brainwork? He proved that every domain of thought produces nothing but the classification of the particular, from experience, towards the general. The mind can therefore only reason concerning the particular, concerning experience, and concerning observed facts. He proved that this, and nothing else, is the effect, the nature of the mind, just as movement is the nature of the body, and that therefore thinking about something supernatural as if it were real (the thing in itself, God, absolute freedom, the eternal personality, absolute spirit, etc.) is just as impossible, just as much in contradiction with the nature of thought, as the representation of a "supernatural piece of sheet-metal"; that the mind is undoubtedly something extraordinary and magnificent, powerful and splendid, but is no more enigmatic and mysterious than any other phenomenon of the universe to those who do not deify it. Dietzgen proved that the mind is comprehensible precisely because the nature of mind consists of understanding, that is, of seeing what is general.(14)

When the proletariat, full of a hunger and a thirst for knowledge, motivated by the desire for freedom and freedom for his class, has understood this, then one could tranquilly state that there is no longer any place in its thoughts where religion could find a place. The capitalist production process, which has given it unemployment, poverty, the need, and the desire for liberation, and finally, knowledge, has caused religion to die in the proletariat. The idea of it has disappeared forever; one does not need a lamp in the full light of day.

Some day, when socialist society exists, nature will be even better understood. The detailed study of society will no longer demand so much sweat and hard work, as it does today. It will lie clear and transparent before our eyes. The idea of religion will no longer be taught to children.

Now we have shown, then, that the conceptions of religion, which in days past played such an important role in the mental life of man, are changed by and with the relations of production. And how much they have changed! The belief in a fetish, in a tree, a river, an animal, the sun, in a deified man of beauty, strength and valor, in a spirit, a father, a sovereign, a ghostly abstraction and, finally. . . . . in nothing. And all these changes constitute a clear consequence of the changes in man's social situation, of his changing relations with nature and with his own species.

First Objection

Our opponents say that the explanations set out above contradict the following point of the social democratic program: religion is a private affair. They consider this point of the program to be hypocrisy and deceitful, intended to win over the believers among the workers by dissimulating our real beliefs. That this was not hypocrisy on our part, but simply a lack of understanding on the part of our enemies, was quite elegantly demonstrated one day in an article by comrade Pannekoek, which we reproduce below:

"The supposedly anti-religious character of social democracy is one of the most persistent misunderstandings used as a weapon against us. No matter how unequivocal our assertions that religion is a private affair, the old accusation is always repeated. It is quite evident that there must be a reason for this; if it was just a matter of a baseless claim, without the least semblance of justification, it would have long ago been revealed to be unsuitable as a weapon and it would have disappeared. For an ignorant person there is a contradiction between our declaration and the fact that, as social democracy grows, religion is disappearing in working-class milieus and that our theory, historical materialism, should contrast so sharply with religious doctrine. This alleged contradiction, which has already disturbed many comrades, has been exploited by our opponents to show that our practical proposal, which leaves the matter of religion to each individual's choice, is nothing but hypocrisy, a pretense to conceal our real anti-religious intentions, and that all of this is really done to win over the religious workers en masse."

"We claim that religion should be the private affair of each individual; that each individual must decide for himself, without anyone else making the decision or prescribing what should be done. This demand emerged as something obvious for the necessities of our practice. For it is completely correct that in this way we have won over, en masse, non-religious and religious workers of various faiths, which means that they want to join together in a common struggle for their class interests. The goal of the social democratic workers movement is nothing less than the economic transformation of society, to make the means of production collective property. It is, then, normal that anything extraneous to this goal should be set aside, along with anything which could lead to disputes among the workers. It would require all the biased narrowness of perspective of the theologians to impute to us, instead of an openly acknowledged goal, another, secret goal, the abolition of religion. Ultimately, one cannot be surprised at the fact that someone who devotes all their thought to religious subtleties and who pays no heed to the deep poverty and the magnificent struggle of the proletarians, should only view the liberating overthrow of a mode of production and the mental and religious changes accompanying it as nothing more than a passage to apostasy and passes over the abolition of poverty, of oppression and of slavery as of no interest."

"Our practical principle in regard to religion was born from the necessity of the practical struggle; as a result, it also must be in accord with our theory, which bases socialism totally on the practice of the everyday struggle. Historical materialism sees in economic relations the basis for all social life; it is always about material necessities, class struggles, of disruptions of the mode of production, where the old ways, and the struggles themselves, exhibit religious discord and conflicts. Religious ideas are nothing but the expressions, the reflections, and the consequences of man's real life relations and, therefore, primarily, of economic institutions.

Today we are also witnessing a thorough economic change but, for the first time in history, the class which must carry it out has a clear understanding that it does not involve the victory of an ideological conception. This clear awareness, which extracts from theory, expresses the practical demand: religion is a private affair!; therefore, this demand is a consequence of both clear scientific consciousness and practical necessity."

"Concerning this conception, that is, the one held about religion by historical materialism, it follows that it can by no means be put in the same bag as bourgeois atheism. The latter is directly opposed and hostile to religion because it saw in religion the theory of the reactionary classes and the principal obstacle to progress. It only saw stupidity and a lack of knowledge and education in religion, which is why it hoped to be able to extirpate the blind faith of the peasants and the stupid petit-bourgeoisie by means of scientific rationalism, especially by means of natural science."

"We, on the other hand, see in religion a necessary product of living conditions, which are essentially of an economic nature. The peasant to whom the caprice of the weather grants a good or a bad harvest, the petit bourgeois for whom the market situation and competition can lead to profit or loss, feel dependent upon mysterious higher powers. Against this immediate sentiment, bookish science, that is, the knowledge that the seasons are determined by natural forces and that the miracles of the Bible are legends invented from whole cloth, is useless. The peasants and the petit bourgeoisie are against this knowledge; it makes them feel uneasy and arouses their mistrust, because it comes from the class that oppresses them and because, as classes in decline, they cannot use it as a weapon, for salvation or even for consolation. They can only imagine consolation in the form of the supernatural, in religious representations."

"It is the just the opposite for the class-conscious proletarian; the cause of his misery lies clearly delineated before him, in the nature of capitalist production and exploitation, which have no supernatural qualities in his eyes. And since a future full of hope is set before him, and he feels that he needs knowledge to be able to break his chains, he passionately seizes upon the study of the social mechanism. His whole worldview, even if he knows nothing about Darwin and Copernicus, is thus a non-religious perspective; he feels the forces with which he must work and struggle as cold secular realities. The irreligiousness of the proletariat is therefore not a consequence of any lesson preached to it, but a direct apprehension of its situation. Reciprocally, this mental disposition born of participation in social struggles leads the workers to diligently appropriate all the rationalist and anti-theological writings of Büchner(15) and Häckel(16) in order to provide a theoretical basis for their way of thinking in the form of the knowledge of natural science. This origin of proletarian atheism results in the fact that the proletariat never employs it as an object of struggle against those who hold different opinions; their only objects of struggle are their social concepts and goals which constitute the essential aspect of their worldview. Proletarians who, as class comrades, live under the same oppression, are their natural comrades-in-arms, even if the effects referred to above are absent among them due to their particular circumstances. For there are such circumstances, abstractions constructed from the power of tradition, which operates everywhere and can only be slowly defeated. The proletarians who work in conditions where powerful, unpredictable, and terrifying natural forces threaten them with death and ruin, such as miners and sailors, often preserve a strong religious sentiment, while they can also be stout fighters against capitalism at the same time. The practical attitude which results from this state of affairs is still frequently underestimated by our party comrades who think that we must oppose Christian belief with our concepts, as 'a superior religion'."

"Thus, in regard to the relation between socialism and religion, the truth is precisely the reverse of the way our theological enemies represent the issue. We do not make the workers renounce their old beliefs by preaching our theory, historical materialism; they lose their beliefs after attentive observation of social relations, which makes them recognize that the abolition of their misery is a goal within their reach. The need to understand these relations more profoundly leads them to study the historical-materialist writings of our great theoreticians. The latter do not exercise their hostility to religion, since there is no longer any belief; to the contrary, they present an appreciation of religion as a historically based phenomenon that will only disappear under future circumstances. This doctrine spares us, then, from having to emphasize ideological differences as if they are what is important, it sets our economic goal on the first level as the only important matter and expresses the latter in the practical demand: religion is a private affair."

Second Objection

Why have old religions continued to exist for so long while old relations of production have had to yield to new ones?

This question must be answered because this fact is utilized by our opponents as an objection against us. The answer is not complicated.

First, an old mode of production does not die all at once. In the preceding centuries, this collapse was taking place quite slowly, and even now, when big industry is so rapidly replacing the old technologies, small business is taking a long time to disappear. Thus, the old religion will still have a place for a long time.

Second, the human mind is lazy. Even when the body already finds itself in new work relations, the mind is slow to adopt new ways of thinking. Tradition, customs, bear upon the mind of living beings. The worker can easily observe this in his surroundings: two men work side by side in the same factory, with the same hardships, the same problems. One, however, is a spiritual invalid who does not want to fight, who is incapable of learning how to think on his own, and who follows the priest's recommendations about politics, religion, and the trade unions. The other worker is full of life, he is all fight; he is always talking, he is ceaselessly making propaganda, constantly agitating, his slogan is: neither God nor Master.

Here, it is tradition, alongside differences in temperament, which is decisive. Catholicism, even though it has managed to manifest itself in new guises, is a religion adapted to ancient relations. Because of the inertia, which is inherent in thought as well as in matter, it stubbornly resists. Long after a mode of production has disappeared one can sometimes still find its dried-up old blossoms.

Thirdly, the rising classes and the threatened classes act in such a way that their old ways of thinking continue for a long time. In other times, when the class struggle was still fought under the guise of religion, under religious slogans, a rising class, which aspired to different social relations than those upheld by the ruling class, often had a new religion which corresponded with what it considered good, just and true. Thus, for example, Calvinism was at first a religion of rebels. But once the rising class replaced the old and became the ruling class, its religion was then transformed into the ruling religion; it was then imposed by force on everyone, but in this way the revolutionary character of the religion was changed into a conservative character; its own new relations were also expressed in this religion. So, Christianity—of old the religion of the poor and the propertyless, and still in that era, simply and unadorned, a religion of love and mutual aid—became, as an official Church, a complicated system of dogmas, ceremonies, representatives of God on Earth, hierarchy, and exploitation, which hardly resembled early Christianity. The class which comes to power and establishes new relations simply changes the nature of religion from a means of struggle to a means of oppression.

And we also see this in our time.

The ruling classes, who demand pleasure for themselves, have inculcated submission, humility, and resigned suffering into the oppressed and used them against them, these aspects of the doctrine of Jesus, after Christianity became the religion of the ruling classes. When the possessing classes were revolutionary, like the Calvinists and the other Protestants, they did not preach tolerance but struggle. But now that a class opposed to them is on the rise, a class which does not want to suffer but to fight until it is victorious, then the old religion of suffering is used again by all sects, even by the ones which were previously revolutionary, in order to separate at least part of the rising classes from the struggle.

It does not surprise us that, because of the cumulative effect of the old relations of production which still subsist, and of tradition and class rule, an old religion should still preserve its existence and its power after so long. And thus, that it no longer has a rich interior life but is rather like fossilized remains, nor should it surprise us now that we know that religion comes from society.

G. Art

We can only briefly touch upon this domain of the mind, because the proletariat, unfortunately, has yet to experience it.

But the fact that our doctrine must be applicable here, and precisely here, can be explained thanks to the following observation and by a single example.

Art is, in its lines, its colors or its tones, the figurative representation of emotional life. Man, only has feelings for man. For this reason, art must change at the same time that the relations between men change.

What follows can serve as an illustration.

The individual of bourgeois society is alone and is ruled by production and its products. This fact must be exemplified in art; from the Greek bourgeois art of the Fifth Century B.C. until now, this has also been demonstrated.

The individual of socialist society has the feeling that he forms a whole with the others, that he has power thanks to them and that he rules production and its products. This will necessarily someday be manifested in his art; this feeling of control, of freedom, of happiness with the whole world must be externalized and will be externalized as sure as the desire for externalization is inherent in social man. But this art will be as different form bourgeois art, that is, enormously different, as the socialist individual will be from the bourgeois individual. And this difference will be brought about—do we need to repeat it once again?—by the fact that the relations of production, which are now based on private ownership and wage labor, will then rest upon collective ownership and labor in common.

VI Conclusion

With what we set forth above we have resolved the question we posed ourselves. Let us examine our conclusions once again.

We have seen that science, law, politics, customs, religion and philosophy, and art change because the relations of production change, which are themselves changed by technological development.

We saw that this was confirmed by a series of quite simple, generally well-known yet all-embracing examples, which involve entire classes and populations.

Obviously, we cannot supply an endless series of examples, and there are undoubtedly many pieces of history which, if we were to be asked to explain them in terms of historical materialism, would put us in an awkward position since we do not know enough about them to explain everything that happens in them to our opponents. But it is precisely for that reason that we have set forth such all-embracing examples, because, if they are correct in their vast scope, the correctness of the theory can hardly be doubted.

Furthermore, historical materialism has been applied by our comrades, primarily in Germany but also in other countries, to every field of history, with such overwhelming success that we can calmly say: experience has demonstrated the correctness of this part of Marxist doctrine.

We have also seen that historical materialism must by no means be considered as a form suitable only for the introduction of historical questions. One must begin by studying. If one wants to know why a class, or a people, thinks in a particular way, one does not say: well, the mode of production was this or that, and therefore this way of thinking was produced. For we would often be mistaken, since the same technology has produced very different ways of thinking in different peoples, just as different modes of production can also be effectively based, among different peoples, on the same technology. Likewise, other factors must be examined, the political history of the people, the climate, the geographical situation, all of which, together with technology, also influence the mode of production and the way of thinking.

Historical materialism, the effect of the productive forces and the relations of production, appears most resplendently highlighted in its environment only when the other factors are understood.

For those who cannot take history courses, and who must be satisfied with the observation of our own epoch, of the struggle between capital and labor, the reflection of which is clearly visible above all in the mind of the worker--and which the worker may quite readily understand by his own efforts thanks to reading good texts and attending good courses.

We have also seen that the various domains of the mind are not sealed compartments. Together they form a single whole, all of them mutually influence one another, politics influences the economy, customs influence politics, technology influences science, and the other way around. There is an interaction, a reaction, a permanent survival of the mental life which flourished in the past. But its motor force is labor, and the channels through which the mental rivers flow are the relations of production.

Tradition is also a force, often a braking force.

The whole process is, as we have seen, a human process, which takes place thanks to man, among men, and in man; that is, it is not a mechanical process. We have been able to repeatedly prove that human need and human instincts are the bases of every event, and that the social instinct is the basis of the instincts of self-preservation and the continuation of the species. Instincts and needs are not mechanical things, they are also mental things, living things, they are feelings, and undoubtedly not at all simply mechanical. We have seen that nothing is more stupid or dishonest than to confuse historical materialism with mechanistic materialism. Technology itself is not just a mechanical process; it is also a mental process.

We have also seen that the great instrument used by nature for furthering the evolution of human thought, struggle, takes the form in our time of class struggle. We have seen, by means of numerous examples, that technology leads the classes into different relations of production and ownership and that, in this way, their ideas aggressively clash with each other; that a struggle among them over ownership results, and at the same time a battle of ideas affecting law, religion, etc.; that the material victory of one class is at the same time the victory of its ideas.

We have seen all of this and we believe we can calmly draw the conclusion that thought constantly changes, that thought is in constant motion, and that in all the domains we have addressed there are no eternal truths, that the only thing that is eternal and absolute is change, evolution. And it is also precisely this general, great truth that, as we said at the beginning of this work, even if we do not subject it to a specific examination, will nonetheless emerge from our experiences. The reader will have observed that we have not set forth this result as a dogma established in advance, but as a consequence of the facts, of simple historical experience.

The Power of the Truth

We have not in any case provided this analysis for the purpose of transforming the workers into philosophers. This will certainly be of interest if the reader understands that the mind, like everything else, is not an absolute thing, but is in a process of transformation; this understanding, as a philosophical truth, however salutary its influence on the mind may be, is still only a secondary outcome.

We have set ourselves another goal; we want to transform the workers into combatants. And into victors. While they attentively read these explanations, they must surely feel their inner power grow.

What, then, is the result of our doctrine and our examples?

If technology changes in such a way that it transforms an insignificant class into a powerful class, a slave into a fighter, then that class's ideas must also be transformed from insignificant to powerful, from servile to proud. And if technology finally transforms this class into a victor, its ideas must finally come to be the only true ones.

Our intention is to give the working class the certainty that it has the truth, and confidence in its mental powers.

For technology is making the proletarian class as numerous as the grains of sand on the seashore; it organizes it, pushes it into battle, transforms it mentally, morally and materially into a powerful class. The old relations of production, private ownership, have proven to be too narrow for modern labor; labor has become social; only with social ownership can it be freely exercised and developed. Technology in the narrow confines of the small business, in the joint-stock companies and the trusts, requires collective ownership so as to be capable of spreading its wings everywhere without obstacles. It does not want to be artificially stimulated at one time, then slowed down at another. And the workers will finally organize technology and the relations of production in accordance with their will, precisely because technology turned them into a powerful class, and because their will expresses the requirements of technology.

But, for just this reason, the ideas of the workers, which rest upon this conviction, to the extent that they rest upon it, are all true. For if reality proves the workers right and, therefore, if the ownership of the means of production is becoming collective, then all their ideas which point in that direction, to the extent that they point in that direction, are also correct and those of their opponents, who do not want this, are mistaken. If, one day, the soil and the machines belong to the whole world, then it is right that it should be that way, and the conception of those who wanted this is revealed to be true; the closer reality comes to this situation, the more true and right is the proletariat's idea of law, and the more false is the conception of its opponents, and in contradiction with reality. And the same is true of its politics. If the workers must become, due to technology, the most numerous, the most organized, the most materially powerful class, their political points of view which express this status are true, and those of their opponents, who oppose this development, are false.

For truth is correspondence between thought and reality.

If the socialism of the working class is a requirement of technology, if, without it, production cannot continue to develop, then the morality of the proletariat, to the extent that it is concerned with this end, is also true morality.

If the working class is right to believe that socialism can only come from the development of the productive forces and from the natural and social forces which have been understood by the working class, then it is also right to not accept anything supernatural, since there is no longer any basis for it, and all its adversaries who subscribe to a religion are imbued with superstitions.

And this is how it is in every domain: the development of technology proceeds in such a way that one class rises or falls not only materially, but also mentally. When the relations sought by a class become reality, its ideas, which expressed its desire for the new relations, then become true. Nor is this surprising, since ideas are nothing but the theories, the considerations, and the summaries of reality in a general concept.

This is why we have attempted with all the forces at our disposal to clarify historical materialism for the workers. The power of the truth must live in the mind of the proletariat.

The Power of the Individual

That last sentence itself leads us to a good conclusion: the power of the truth must live in the mind of the worker.

Surely, technology is leading to socialism. We do not make history by our own will.

"Labor is becoming social." "The relations of production must become socialist." "Property relations demand socialization."

It is true. Social matters are more powerful than the mind of the individual. The individual must follow wherever it leads him.

But technology is composed of machines and of men. Labor in production means human hands, human brains and human hearts which take part in it. Property relations are relations between owners and non-owners.

Once again: the process is a living process. The social power which drags us along is not a dead fate, a brutal mass of compact matter. It is society, it is a living force.

To speak truly, we must go in the direction it is going in. The labor process is dragging us in a direction that we have not ourselves determined. We do not make history by our own will.

But . . . we do make it.

It is not a blind destiny but living society which destines you, workers, to usher in socialism.

You, as a class, can do nothing else. You must want higher wages, a happier life, and more leisure. You must organize. You must fight the State, you must conquer political power, and you must be victorious. It is production, it is living labor that you want.

But does it not also depend upon you personally to bring this about quickly, smoothly and correctly? Is it not precisely because you must do so as a living power that it will depend upon you, living individuals, living men, women and children, not what you do, but how you do it?

This depends on your body and your mind.

Physically robust and mentally strong proletarians will realize one of the most magnificent and greatest tasks ever seen in the world better than weak proletarians.

Under capitalism, to be as physically as healthy as you will need to be does not depend on your desires. Wage levels, the length of the working day, housing, do not depend on you alone. But to a very high degree, it is up to you whether or not you are mentally healthy. You can fully and completely accept into your mind the power and the force of the truth, of the socialist social truth, even when your body is not so strong.

It is something characteristic of the mind. Social existence dominates it in such a way that it can be feeble, tired, mortally exhausted, that it can no longer move.

But technology awakens it, shows it a point of light on the horizon, happiness, a goal. It points the way to victory for the class through social existence, then the mind of those who belong to that class go into motion; then it is impassioned, it lives, it aspires to something, it acts, then the saying according to which the mind rules the body becomes true. The mind then becomes more than the body; however weak the body may be, however under-nourished, however anemic, with a thousand troubles and worries, the mind becomes powerful, the mind becomes free.

Worker, comrade, it is necessary for you to be told that your mind can be free under capitalism. The process of production can make you mentally free immediately. You must free yourself from the mental yoke of the bourgeoisie. Historical materialism teaches you about the relation between man and nature. It teaches you that the time approaches when not only will humanity rule nature but will also rule itself. It teaches you that you are called upon to hasten the arrival of that day. He who understands this and acts in accordance with this understanding is mentally free. Only he, with his individual power, is capable of helping to lead his class to the new society.

The mind must be revolutionized. It must extirpate prejudice and cowardice. The most important thing is mental propaganda. Knowledge, mental power, is the essential thing, the most necessary of all.

Only knowledge creates a good organization, a good trade union movement, correct policies and therefore improvements in the fields of economics and politics.

No prosperity will be possible as long as capitalism exists.

Only socialism will bring prosperity.

But socialism can only be achieved & the hard fight for socialism can only be led, by mentally energetic men who are intellectually free.

First make your own mind strong, and then to do so with the minds of your comrades: this is the great and universal power of the individual, thanks to which he can hasten the advent of the socialist future.

Try it, workers, comrades. Drink deep from the development of the productive forces which you have before your eyes and even in your hands, what you must find in them: the new truth, the socialist vision of the world. And spread it!

Notes

3. Dreiklassenwahlrecht: in this voting system introduced by Frederick Wilhelm IV in Prussia in 1849 and which was in effect in that State until 1918, the lower chamber (Landtag) was elected by indirect universal suffrage, but the higher chamber was divided into three estates and representation in this chamber was proportional to the taxes paid by the three estates, so that more than 80% of the electorate elected less than one third of the deputies. (Note from the French translation)

4. Norddeutsche Bund: a Federation of 22 German States located north of the Main, created on Bismarck's initiative after Prussia's victory over Austria, and implemented in 1867.

5. We cannot sufficiently recommend to the reader, especially the working class reader, Kautsky's lecture on Ethics and the Materialist Conception of History. Ethics is the last wall behind which people who want to keep the worker in a state of childhood thanks to religion are entrenched. When the terrestrial origin of the highest moral precepts is clarified, many mental obstacles are overcome. So also solidarity will be reinforced if it is understood to have its origin in the most ancient sentiments of the human species.

6. Abraham Kuyper (1837-1920): professor of theology, he helped found the Amsterdam Free University; as a journalist, he founded two newspapers, De Standaard and De Heraut, and as a politician, he was one of the founders of the Anti-Revolutionary Party and was Prime Minister of the Netherlands from 1901 to 1905. (Note from the French translation)

7. Two mental tendencies are possible for the bourgeois or capitalist politician, who, as a result of the development of technology and the mode of production, comes into conflict with the working class. He can confess that he cannot and does not follow the precepts of the highest morality in regard to the working class. He then becomes a cynic, he mutes the voice inside him that

tells him what he himself knows is "right" with a "this won't work". Or else he says that he recognizes and follows the highest morality. In that case he becomes a hypocrite whose words and actions are in sharp contradiction with each other, who dissimulates his anti-social actions behind beautiful resonant words. And the hypocrite is especially repugnant when, as in the case of Kuyper, he associates religion and devotion with his hypocrisy. Such phenomena, however, are not personal sins but, as we have shown, a necessary consequence of the development of the productive forces.

8. Two mental tendencies are possible, both among the capitalists and their political representatives as well as among the workers and their representatives. The worker could take nothing into account except the everyday struggle. His moral sentiment is then limited to a narrow circle, to his colleagues in his trade, for example. Or he could above all have his sights set on the final goal, socialism. In that case his moral sentiment embraces the whole proletariat, and can also come to include all of humanity. Cynicism and hypocrisy are the two general phenomena necessary in the ruling class; in the ruled class, an uninspiring narrowness and revolutionary enthusiasm. There are naturally many intermediate stages between the two poles.

9. Our opponents occasionally conclude from this that we think that anything is always permitted against the capitalists. This is false. As we said above, this is only the case when it is necessary for the veritable salvation of our class. The application of such means would be exactly contrary to the morality which orders us to act in the interest of our class.

10. It is often said that this abrupt representation and this acknowledgment of the existence of a class morality is prejudicial to our propaganda, because our opponents exploit these things against us and thus arouse the suspicions of the ignorant masses against us. But whoever says this is unaware of the power that theoretical truth confers upon a revolutionary class.

In regard to practice, I can recommend, based on my experience as an agitator, the following in response to this claim. When an opponent reproaches us for recognizing the existence of a class morality – since it is not a question of preaching a class morality – demand that he make reference to particular instances where our class lied, deceived, etc. In most cases he will not be able to produce much in the way of evidence; if he cites the case of the theft of a secret document, explain to your listeners the whole case. If your listeners are workers who are ripe for our agitation, then the sentiment of solidarity with their comrades, which is inherited from our predecessors, will immediately be instinctively voiced within them, and they will feel that we are right.

If the opponent's attack is repulsed in this way, then go on the offensive. After the failure to prove the existence of a bad class morality among us, show the bad class morality of the capitalists, of the yellow trade unions, of the bourgeois press, and of the politicians, as it is directed against us, against the oppressed class. Go on to compare our class morality, which defends the oppressed, and their class morality, which seeks to repress them; compare capitalist society, which implies such a morality, with the classless socialist society in which all humanity forms a solidaric brotherhood. Only then will you have an effect on the workers. And once again it will become clear that only theoretical truth will lead us to victory.

11. Today, as well, when commodity society penetrates primitive peoples, they are also "converted" to monotheism.

12. Only the Italian cities remained Catholic, also for economic reasons. The power of the Pope signified the power of Italy over the Christian world.

13. For reasons of space we naturally cannot deal with every philosophical system.

14. Wage Labor and Capital, Karl Marx.

15. The Communist Manifesto, Karl Marx and Friedrich Engels.

16. Marx examined how the relations of production modify the content of thought. But thinking itself is explained by bourgeois philosophers and theologians as something that comes from God. Thus, after Marx's critique of the content of thinking, consequently there still remained an unexplained part of the world of ideas which the bourgeoisie could use to buttress their own status and to put down the proletariat. This is the part that Joseph Dietzgen studied. As Marx had covered the material side, Dietzgen approached the problem from the other side, that of the idea. Whereas Marx set forth what social matter does to the mind, Dietzgen showed what the mind itself does. Marx often heard the bourgeoisie say: "But no one can understand the nature of things; the nature of things is beyond or above the capacities of our imagination." This is how they tried to preserve the supernatural. Dietzgen proved that the cause of the incomprehensibility of the nature of things for the bourgeoisie does not reside in things themselves, but in their own understanding. The bourgeoisie, the bourgeois philosophers and theologians, do not understand what it means to understand something. Dietzgen explained to the workers what understanding is, and therefore, thanks to Marx and Dietzgen, the entire relation between thought and social existence has been made clear, since one studied the modifications of thought, and the other the nature of thought.

Marx himself had absorbed his knowledge about society from the class struggle of the proletariat which was taking place before his eyes in England and France. Dietzgen formed his conceptions of the mind on the basis of Marx's knowledge of society. He was able to discern historical materialism in Marx's writings, and only thus could Dietzgen arrive at his transparent doctrine of the mind. Both of them, then, derived their knowledge from the class struggle of the proletariat. The proletariat gave them, through their labor, their demands and their associations, the experience, and they constructed the doctrine, the theory. One could say that they gave back to the proletariat a hundred-fold what they had taken from it.

17. This apparently refers to Friedrich Büchner (born 1824), a German naturalist and materialist philosopher, author of Force and Matter (1855) and Nature and Mind (1857). Büchner was a popularizer and polemicist who championed the experimental method of science. (Note from the French translation)

18. Ernst Häckel (1834-1919), German biologist and philosopher, was a stalwart proponent of the theory of evolution and popularized Darwin's work in Germany. He is also considered to be the father of ecology. Some believe he was one of the first to engage in racial classification, since he established a racial hierarchy within an evolutionist framework and was therefore a precursor of the Nazi's political-biological doctrine. (Note from the French translation)